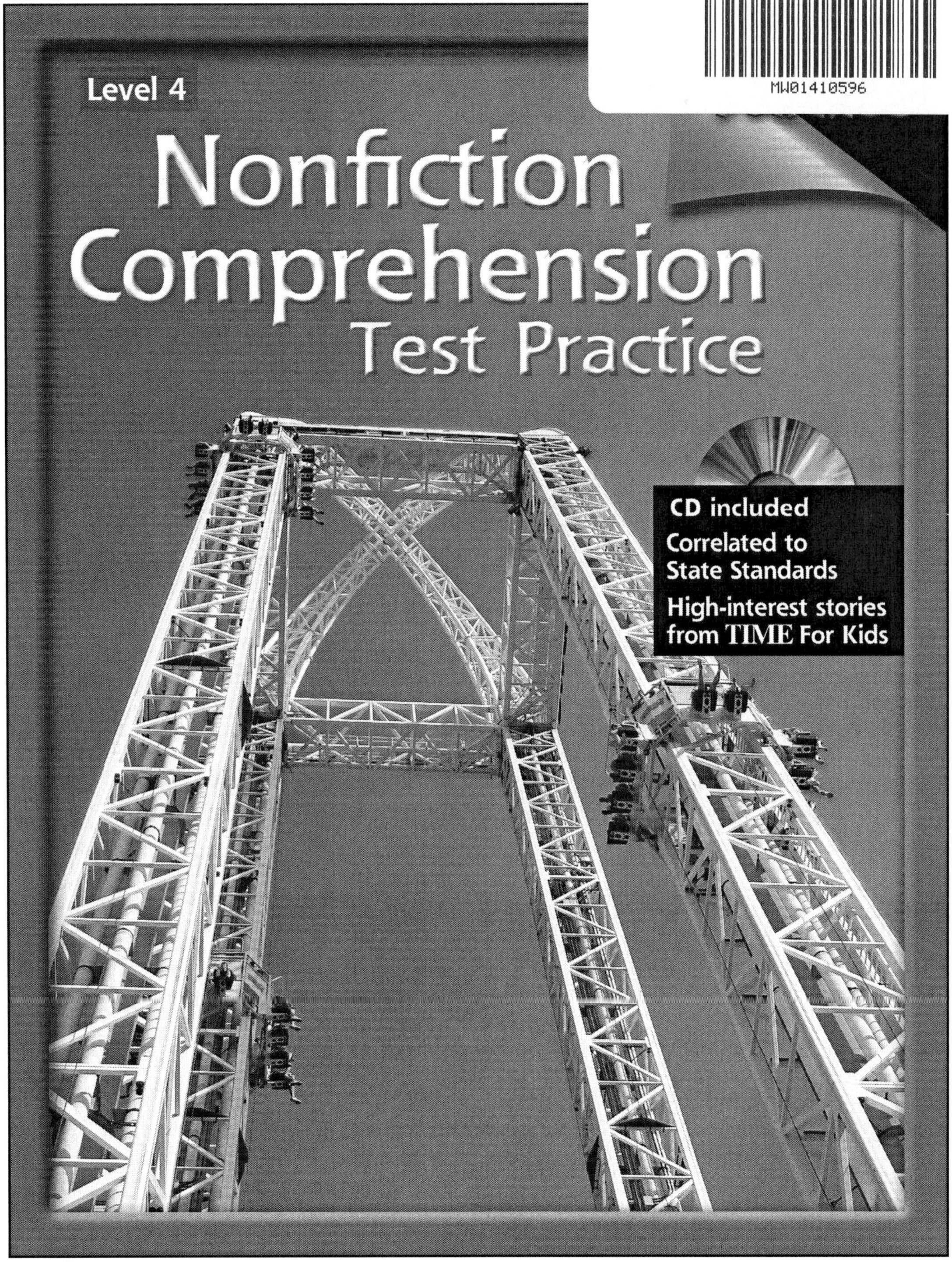

Level 4

Nonfiction Comprehension Test Practice

CD included
Correlated to State Standards
High-interest stories from TIME For Kids

Author
Jennifer Overend Prior, M.Ed.
Introduction by Kathleen Lewis, M.A.

Project Developer
Edward Fry, Ph.D.

Reading Passages provided by T*IME* *For Kids* magazine

Editors

Jennifer Overend Prior, M.Ed.
Wanda Kelly, M.A.

Editorial Project Manager

Lori Kamola, M.S.Ed.

Editor-in-Chief

Sharon Coan, M.S.Ed.

Cover Artist

Neri Garcia

Product Manager

Phil Garcia

Publisher

Corinne Burton, M.A.Ed.

Shell Education
5301 Oceanus Drive
Huntington Beach, CA 92649-1030
http://www.shelleducation.com
ISBN-978-1-4258-0425-1
© 2006 Shell Educational Publishing, Inc.
Reprinted 2013

The classroom teacher may reproduce copies of materials in this book for classroom use only. The reproduction of any part for an entire school or school system is strictly prohibited. No part of this publication may be transmitted, stored, or recorded in any form without written permission from the publisher.

Table of Contents

Standards Correlations 4

Introduction 5

Lesson 1: A Lucky Brake 21

Lesson 2: A Sticky Situation 27

Lesson 3: Marathon Madness 33

Lesson 4: Do Girls Know Best? 39

Lesson 5: Hot on Lewis and Clark's Trail 45

Lesson 6: A New Dino Duo 51

Lesson 7: LEGOLAND 57

Lesson 8: The Poetry Express 63

Lesson 9: Hooked! 69

Lesson 10: Peanut Problems 75

Lesson 11: Looking Out for the Gators 81

Lesson 12: Bye-Bye, Beanies? 87

Lesson 13: Tower of Thrills 93

Lesson 14: Bullies in the Park! 99

Lesson 15: Policeman Next Door 105

Lesson 16: Monster of the Deep 111

Lesson 17: Feel the Force 117

Lesson 18: Goosebumps TV 123

Lesson 19: A Review of Harry Potter and the Sorcerer's Stone 129

Lesson 20: Captivity Equals Cruelty for Whales 135

Answer Key 141

Answer Sheet 144

(**Note:** Each six-part lesson revolves around an article from *Time For Kids*. The article titles are listed here for you to choose topics that will appeal to your students, but the individual articles do not begin on the first page of the lessons. The lessons in this book may be done in any order.)

©Shell Educational Publishing   #10334 Nonfiction Comprehension Test Practice

Standards Correlations

Shell Education is committed to producing educational materials that are research- and standards-based. In this effort we have correlated all of our products to the academic standards of all 50 states, the District of Columbia, and the Department of Defense Dependent Schools. You can print a correlation report customized for your state directly from our website at **http://www.shelleducation.com.**

Purpose and Intent of Standards

The No Child Left Behind legislation mandates that all states adopt academic standards that identify the skills students will learn in kindergarten through grade twelve. While many states had already adopted academic standards prior to NCLB, the legislation set requirements to ensure the standards were detailed and comprehensive.

Standards are designed to focus instruction and guide adoption of curricula. Standards are statements that describe the criteria necessary for students to meet specific academic goals. They define the knowledge, skills, and content students should acquire at each level. Standards are also used to develop standardized tests to evaluate students' academic progress.

In many states today, teachers are required to demonstrate how their lessons meet state standards. State standards are used in development of all of our products, so educators can be assured they meet the academic requirements of each state. Complete standards correlation reports for each state can be printed directly from our website as well.

How to Find Standards Correlations

To print a correlation report for this product, visit our website at **http://www.shelleducation.com** and follow the on-screen directions. If you require assistance in printing correlation reports, please contact Customer Service at 1-877-777-3450.

Introduction

Why Every Teacher Needs This Book

In a day of increased accountability and standards-based instruction, teachers are feeling greater pressure for their students to perform well on standardized tests. Every teacher knows that students who can read, and comprehend what they read, will have better test performance.

In many classrooms today, teachers experience challenges they are not trained to meet, including limited English speakers, students with disabilities, high student mobility rates, and student apathy. Many states with poor standardized test scores have students that come from print-poor environments. Teachers need help developing competent readers and students who can apply their knowledge in the standardized test setting.

The *Nonfiction Comprehension Test Practice* series is a tool that will help teachers to teach comprehension skills to their students and enable their students to perform better in a test setting. This series supplies motivating, readable, interesting, nonfiction text, and comprehension exercises to help students practice comprehension skills while truly becoming better readers. The activities can be quick or in depth, allowing students to practice skills daily. What is practiced daily will be acquired by students. Practice for standardized tests needs to be started at the beginning of the school year, not a few weeks before the tests. The articles in this series are current and develop knowledge about today's world as well as the past. Students will begin thinking, talking, and developing a framework of knowledge which is crucial for comprehension.

When a teacher sparks an interest in knowledge, students will become life-long learners. In the process of completing these test practice activities, not only will you improve your students' test scores, you will create better readers and life-long learners.

Readability

All of the articles used in this series have been edited for readability. The Fry Graph, The Dale-Chall Readability Formula, or the Spache Readability Formula was used depending on the level of the article. Of more than 100 predictive readability formulas, these are the most widely used. These formulas count and factor in three variables: the number of words, syllables, and sentences. The Dale-Chall and Spache formulas also use vocabulary lists. The Dale-Chall Formula is typically used for upper-elementary and secondary grade-level materials. It uses its own vocabulary list and takes into account the total number of words and sentences. The formula reliably gives the readability for the chosen text. The Spache Formula is vocabulary-based, paying close attention to the percentage of words not present in the formula's vocabulary list. This formula is best for evaluating primary and early elementary texts. Through the use of these formulas, the levels of the articles are appropriate and comprehensible for students at each grade level.

Introduction (cont.)

General Lesson Plan

At each grade level of this series, there are 20 articles that prove interesting and readable to students. Each article is followed by questions on the following topics:

Sentence comprehension—Five true/false statements are related back to one sentence from the text.

Word study—One word from the text is explained (origin, part of speech, unique meaning, etc.). Activities can include completion items (cloze statements), making illustrations, or compare-and-contrast items.

Paragraph comprehension—This section contains one paragraph from the text and five multiple-choice questions directly related to that paragraph. The questions range from drawing information directly from the page to forming opinions and using outside knowledge.

Whole-story comprehension—Eight multiple-choice questions relate back to the whole article or a major part of it. They can include comprehension that is factual, is based on opinion, involves inference, uses background knowledge, involves sequencing or classifying, relates to cause and effect, and involves understanding the author's intent. All levels of reading comprehension are covered.

Enrichment for language mechanics and expression—This section develops language mechanics and expression through a variety of activities.

Graphic development—Graphic organizers that relate to the article are used to answer a variety of comprehension questions. In some lessons, students create their own maps, graphs, and diagrams that relate to the article.

The following is a list of words from the lessons that may be difficult for some students. These words are listed here so that you may review them with your students as needed.

Word	Page	Word	Page	Word	Page
hyphen	21	Meriwether	45	allergic	75
Missouri	23	Ankylosaur	51	egrets	82
eureka	29	Cretaceous	52	ibis	82
sauntered	31	paleontologist	53	phosphorus	83
onomatopoeia	33	Tyrannosaurus	53	ferocious	85
marathon	34	Nodosaurid	53	billionaire	88
simile	37	browser	61	rhetorical	97
camaraderie	39	graffiti	63	Pilanesberg	101
embarrassed	40	alliteration	67	Minke	139
quotations	43	denotation	73		

Introduction (cont.)

What Do Students Need to Learn?

Successful reading requires comprehension. Comprehending means having the ability to connect words and thoughts to knowledge already possessed. If you have little or no knowledge of a subject, it is difficult to comprehend an article or text written on that subject. Comprehension requires motivation and interest. Once your students start acquiring knowledge, they will want to fill in the gaps and learn more.

In order to help students be the best readers they can be, a teacher needs to be familiar with what students need to know to comprehend well. A teacher needs to know Bloom's levels of comprehension, traditional comprehension skills and expected products, and the types of questions that are generally used on standardized comprehension tests, as well as methods that can be used to help students build a framework for comprehension.

Bloom's Taxonomy

In 1956, Benjamin Bloom created a classification for questions that are commonly used to demonstrate comprehension. These levels are listed here along with the corresponding skills that will demonstrate understanding. These skills are important to remember when teaching comprehension to assure that students have attained higher levels of comprehension. Use this classification to form your own questions whenever students read or listen to literature.

> **Knowledge**—Students will recall information. They will show knowledge of dates, events, places, and main ideas. Questions will include words such as: *who, what, where, when, list, identify,* and *name.*
>
> **Comprehension**—Students will understand information. They will compare and contrast, order, categorize, and predict consequences. Questions will include words such as: *compare, contrast, describe, summarize, predict,* and *estimate.*
>
> **Application**—Students will use information in new situations. Questions will include words such as: *apply, demonstrate, solve, classify,* and *complete.*
>
> **Analysis**—Students will see patterns. They will be able to organize parts and figure out meaning. Questions will include words such as: *order, explain, arrange,* and *analyze.*
>
> **Synthesis**—Students will use old ideas to create new ones. They will generalize, predict, and draw conclusions. Questions will include words such as: *what if, rewrite, rearrange, combine, create,* and *substitute.*
>
> **Evaluation**—Students will compare ideas and assess value. They will make choices and understand a subjective viewpoint. Questions will include words such as: *assess, decide,* and *support your opinion.*

Introduction (cont.)

Comprehension Skills

There are many skills that form the complex activity of comprehension. This wide range of understandings and abilities develops over time in competent readers. The following list includes many traditional skills found in scope and sequence charts and standards for reading comprehension.

- identifies details
- recognizes stated main idea
- follows directions
- determines sequence
- recalls details
- locates reference
- recalls gist of story
- labels parts
- summarizes
- recognizes anaphoric relationships
- identifies time sequence
- describes a character
- retells story in own words
- infers main idea
- infers details
- infers cause and effect
- infers author's purpose/intent
- classifies, places into categories
- compares and contrasts
- draws conclusions
- makes generalizations
- recognizes paragraph (text) organization
- predicts outcome
- recognizes hyperbole and exaggeration
- experiences empathy for a character
- experiences an emotional reaction to the text
- judges quality/appeal of text
- judges author's qualifications
- recognizes facts vs. opinions
- applies understanding to a new situation
- recognizes literary style
- recognizes figurative language
- identifies mood
- identifies plot and story line

Introduction (cont.)

Observable Comprehension Products

There are many exercises that students can complete when they comprehend the material they read. Some of these products can be performed orally in small groups. Some lend themselves more to independent paper-and-pencil type activities. Although there are more, the following are common and comprehensive products of comprehension.

Recognizing—underlining, multiple choice items, matching, true/false statements

Recalling—writing a short answer, filling in the blanks, flashcard question and answer

Paraphrasing—retelling in own words, summarizing

Classifying—grouping components, naming clusters, completing comparison tables, ordering components on a scale

Following directions—completing steps in a task, using a recipe, constructing

Visualizing—graphing, drawing a map, illustrating, making a time line, creating a flow chart

Fluent reading—accurate pronunciation, phrasing, intonation, dramatic qualities

Reading Comprehension Questions

Teaching the kinds of questions that appear on standardized tests gives students the framework to anticipate and thus look for the answers to questions while reading. This framework will not only help students' scores, but it will actually help them learn how to comprehend what they are reading. Some of the types of questions students will find on standardized comprehension tests are as follows:

Vocabulary—These questions are based on word meaning, common words, proper nouns, technical words, geographical words, and unusual adjectives.

Facts—These questions ask exactly what was written, using *who, what, when, where, why, how,* and *how many.*

Sequence—These questions are based on order—what happened first, last, and in between.

Conditionals—These questions use qualifying terms such as: *if, could, alleged,* etc.

Summarizing—These questions require students to restate, choose main ideas, conclude, and create a new title. Also important here is for students to understand and state the author's purpose.

Outcomes—These questions often involve readers drawing upon their own experiences or bringing outside knowledge to the composition. Students must understand cause and effect, results of actions, and implications.

Opinion—These questions ask the author's intent and mood and require use of background knowledge to answer.

Introduction (cont.)

Graphic Organizers

Reading and comprehension can be easier for students with a few simple practices. For top comprehension, students need a wide vocabulary, ideas about the subject they are reading, and understanding of the structure of the text. Pre-reading activities will help students in all of these areas. Graphic organizers help students build vocabulary, brainstorm ideas, and understand the structure of the text.

Graphic organizers aid students with vocabulary and comprehension. Graphic organizers can help students comprehend more and, in turn, gain insight into how to comprehend in future readings. This process teaches a student a way to connect new information to prior knowledge that is stored in his or her brain. Different types of graphic organizers are listed below by category.

Concept organizers include: semantic maps, spider maps (word webs), Venn diagrams, and fishbone diagrams.

Semantic map—This organizer builds vocabulary. A word for study is placed in the center of the page, and four categories are made around it. The categories expand on the nature of the word and relate it back to personal knowledge and experience of the students.

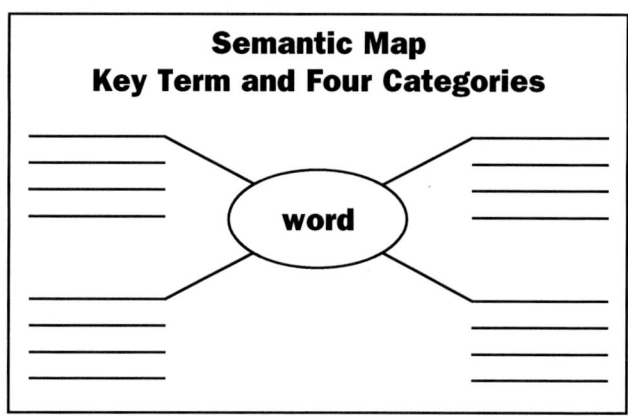

Spider map (word web)—The topic, concept, or theme is placed in the middle of the page. Like a spider's web, thoughts and ideas come out from the center, beginning with main ideas and flowing out to details.

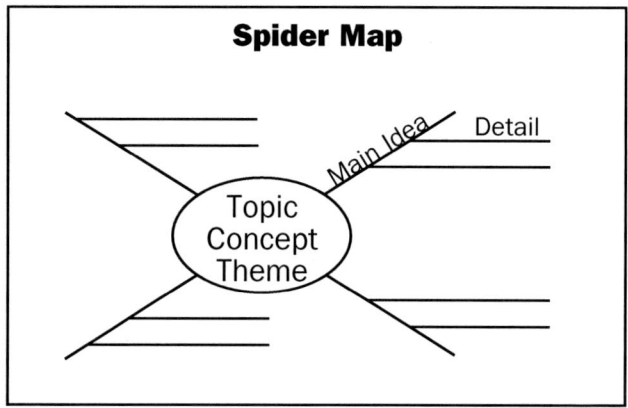

Introduction (cont.)

Graphic Organizers (cont.)

Venn diagram—This organizer compares and contrasts two ideas. With two large circles intersecting, each circle represents a different topic. The area of each circle that does not intersect is for ideas and concepts that are only true about one topic. The intersection is for ideas and concepts that are true about both topics.

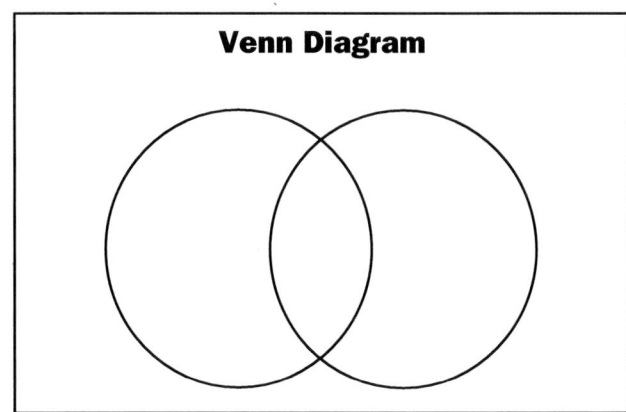

Fishbone diagram—This organizer deals with cause and effect. The result is listed first, branching out in a fishbone pattern with the causes that lead up to the result, along with other effects that happened along the way.

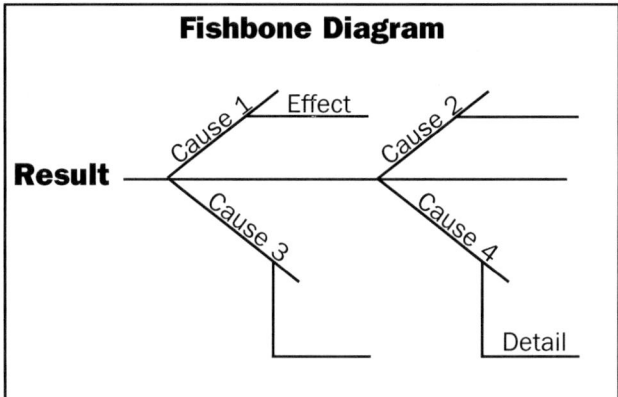

Continuum organizers can be linear or circular and contain a chain of events. These include time lines, chain of events, multiple linear maps, and circular or repeating maps.

Time lines—Whether graphing ancient history or the last hour, time lines help students to see how events have progressed and understand patterns in history.

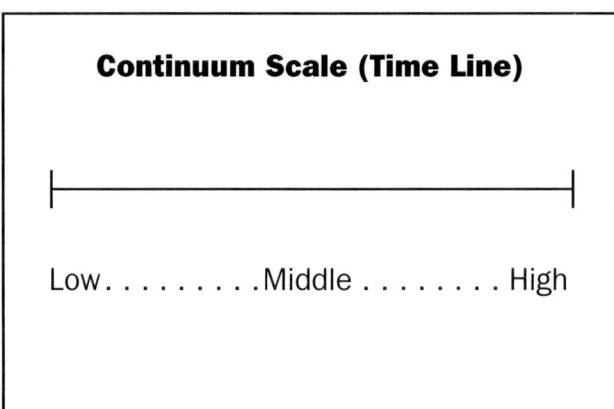

Introduction (cont.)

Graphic Organizers (cont.)

Chain of events—This organizer not only shows the progression of time but also emphasizes cause and effect. Beginning with the initiating event inside of a box, subsequent arrows and boxes follow showing the events in order.

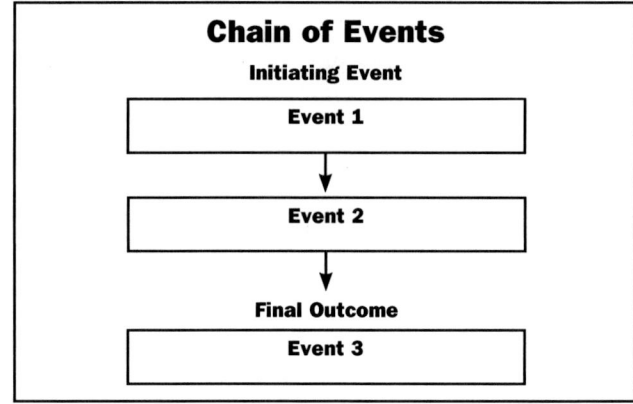

Multiple linear maps—These organizers can help students visualize how different events can be happening at the same time, either in history or in a story, and how those events affect each other.

Circular or repeating maps—These organizers lend themselves to events that happen in a repeating pattern like events in science, such as the water cycle.

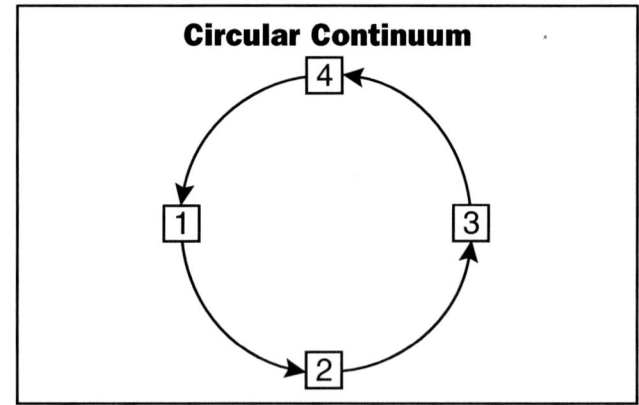

Hierarchical organizers show structure. These include: network trees, structured overviews, and class/example and properties maps. These organizers help students begin to visualize and comprehend hierarchy of knowledge, going from the big picture to the details.

Network tree—This organizer begins with a main, general topic. From there it branches out to examples of that topic, further branching out with more and more detail.

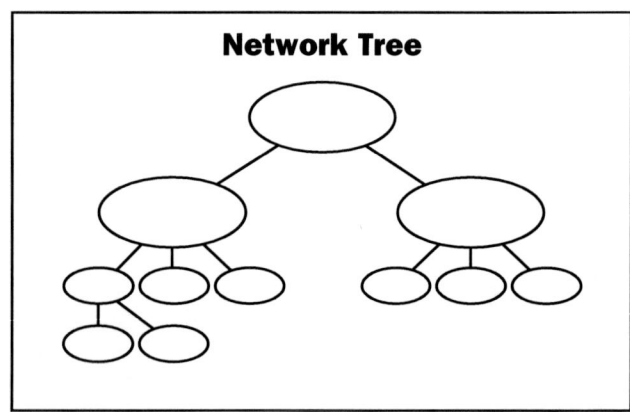

Introduction (cont.)

Graphic Organizers (cont.)

Structured overview—This is very similar to a network tree, but it varies in that it has a very structured look.

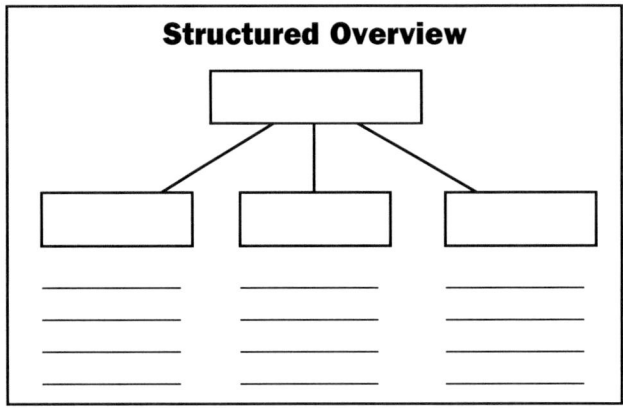

Class/example and properties map—Organized graphically, this map gives the information of class, example, and properties.

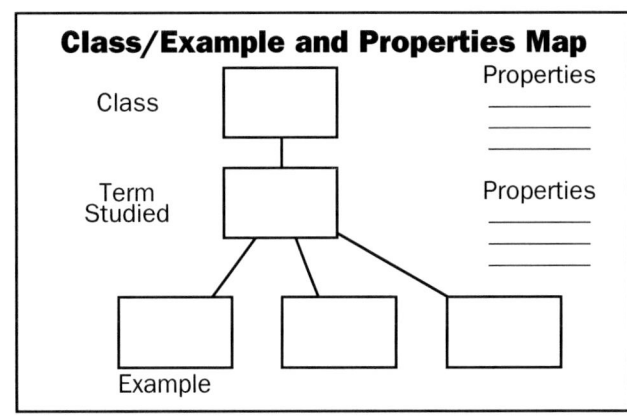

Spreadsheets are important organizers today. Much computer information is stored on spreadsheets. It is important for students to learn how to create, read, and comprehend these organizers. These include semantic feature analysis, compare and contrast matrices, and simple spreadsheet tables.

Semantic feature analysis—This organizer gives examples of a topic and lists features. A plus or a minus indicates if that example possesses those features.

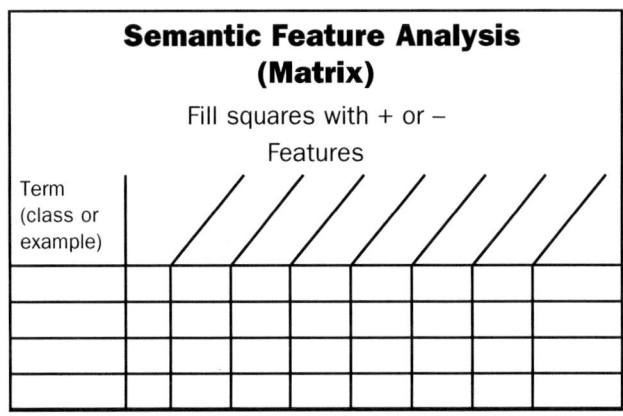

Introduction (cont.)

Graphic Organizers (cont.)

Compare and contrast matrix—This organizer compares and contrasts two or more examples of different attributes.

Compare/Contrast Matrix (Spreadsheets)		
Attribute 1		
Attribute 2		
Attribute 3		

Simple spreadsheet table—Much information can be visualized through spreadsheets or tables. Choose examples and qualities and arrange them in spreadsheet style.

Maps are helpful in understanding spatial relationships. There are geographical maps, but there are also street maps and floor plans.

Geographical map—These organizers can range from globes to cities, and details are limited.

Street map—Information on this type of organizer becomes more detailed.

Floor plan—This organizer becomes more detailed, from a building to a room or a student's desk.

Numerical graphs such as bar graphs, pie charts, and tables become important in comprehension, too.

Bar graph—With a vertical and a horizontal axis, this graph shows a comparison between subjects. It is important to be able to draw the correct information out of it.

Pie chart—In the circular shape of a pie, amounts totaling 100% are shown as pieces of pie. Once again, drawing correct information is important.

Table—Information is organized into rows and columns to display relationships. A table can help to recognize patterns in a given problem.

Using graphic organizers while reading class material will help students know what to do in order to better comprehend material on standardized comprehension tests. A varied use of all types of organizers will help students of different learning styles hit a method that works for them.

Pre-reading Strategies

It is widely understood that for comprehension and acquisition to take place, new information must be integrated with what the reader knows. Pre-reading strategies will help students to build knowledge and restructure the information they already possess in order to more fully comprehend what they are reading. After a teacher has spent time teaching pre-reading strategies, students will know what to do when reading on their own.

Introduction *(cont.)*

Building Vocabulary

Common sense reveals that there is a symbiotic relationship between knowledge of vocabulary and comprehension. Vocabulary development and comprehension span the curriculum. Students come across a large and diverse vocabulary in science, social science, mathematics, art, and even physical education. Skills and strategies for understanding vocabulary can be taught throughout the day. You can build your students' vocabulary directly and/or indirectly. Both ways have shown merit for different learners, so a combination will be sure to help all of the learners in your classroom.

Whether done directly or indirectly, teaching the kind of vocabulary that occurs in a text will greatly improve comprehension. Teaching vocabulary directly, a teacher would list the vocabulary in the text and have the students find the definitions in some manner. Indirectly, a teacher would introduce the content of the text and then elicit vocabulary that the students bring with them on the subject. The use of graphic organizers is helpful in doing this. (See pages 10–14 for different types.) The teacher would lead the discussion to specific words if necessary.

Direct teaching—The more conventional way of teaching vocabulary has its merits. Give students a list of vocabulary words and then they can look them up. This method teaches the use of reference materials and can be a good way to learn vocabulary. However, students truly learn vocabulary when they are involved in the construction of meaning rather than simply memorizing definitions.

Incidental or indirect teaching—This is really a combination of direct teaching and incidental learning for the well-equipped teacher. Teaching in this fashion, a teacher uses the students' knowledge and interests to begin a vocabulary development session that will end with what he or she wants the students to learn. Along the way, the teacher builds a grand vocabulary list and student interest. Also, students buy into the fact that they are part of the process and that learning vocabulary can be a personal experience that they can control. The students will learn how to become independent learners, studying things that interest them.

A general approach to building vocabulary could include the following:

Semantic association—Students brainstorm a list of words associated with a familiar word, sharing everyone's knowledge of vocabulary and discussing the less familiar words.

Semantic mapping—Once the brainstorming is done, students can group the words into categories, creating a visual organization to understand relationships.

Semantic feature analysis—Another way to group words is according to certain features. Use a chart to show similarities and differences between words.

Analogies—This practice will further help students to see the relationships of words. Also, analogies are often used on standardized tests. (e.g., Doctor is to patient as teacher is to __student__.)

Word roots and origins—The study of these, as well as affixes, will help students to deduce new words. Students can ask themselves, "Does it look like a word I know? Can I figure out the meaning in the given context?"

Introduction (cont.)

Building Vocabulary (cont.)

Synonyms and antonyms—The study of these related words provides a structure for meaning and is also good practice for learning and building vocabulary.

Brainstorming—The use of graphic organizers to list and categorize ideas will help greatly with comprehension. A great way to get started is with a KWL chart. By listing ideas that are known, what students want to know, and, when finished, what they learned, relationships will be established so that comprehension and acquisition of knowledge will take place. Word webs work well, too. Anticipating the types of words and ideas that will appear in the text will help with fluency of reading as well as with comprehension.

Understanding Structure

To be able to make predictions and find information in writing, a student must understand structure. From the structure of a sentence to a paragraph to an essay, this skill is important and sometimes overlooked in instruction. Some students have been so immersed in literature that they have a natural understanding of structure. For instance, they know that a fairy tale starts out "Once upon a time . . . ," has a good guy and a bad guy, has a problem with a solution, and ends ". . . happily ever after." But when a student does not have this prior knowledge, making heads or tails of a fairy tale is difficult. The same holds true with not understanding that the first sentence of a paragraph will probably contain the main idea, followed with examples of that idea. When looking back at a piece to find the answer to a question, understanding structure will allow students to quickly scan the text for the correct area in which to find the information. Furthermore, knowing where a text is going to go structurally will help prediction as well as comprehension.

Building a large vocabulary is important for comprehension, but comprehension and acquisition also require a framework for relating new information to what is already in the brain. Students must be taught the structure of sentences and paragraphs. Knowing the structure of these, they will begin to anticipate and predict what will come next. Not having to decode every word reduces the time spent reading a sentence and thus helps students remember what they read at the beginning of the sentence. Assessing an author's purpose and quickly recalling a graphic or framework of personal knowledge will help a reader predict and anticipate what vocabulary and ideas might come up in an article or story.

Several activities will help with understanding structure. The following list offers some ideas to help students:

Write—A great way to understand structure is to use it. Teach students the proper structure when they write.

Color code—When reading a text, students can use colored pencils, highlighter markers, or crayons to color code certain elements such as main idea, supporting sentences, and details. Once the colors are in place, they can study and tell in their own words about paragraph structure.

Introduction *(cont.)*

Understanding Structure *(cont.)*

Go back in the text—Discuss a comprehension question with students. Ask them, "What kinds of words are you going to look for in the text to find the answer? Where are you going to look for them?" (The students should pick main ideas in the question and look for those words in the topic sentences of the different paragraphs.)

Graphic organizers—Use the list of graphic organizers (pages 10–14) to find one that will suit your text. Have students create an organizer as a class, in a small group, or with a partner.

Study common order—Students can also look for common orders. Types of orders can include chronological, serial, logical, functional, spatial, and hierarchical.

Standardized Tests

Standardized tests have taken a great importance in education today. As an educator, you know that standardized tests do not necessarily provide an accurate picture of a student. There are many factors that do not reflect the students' competence that sway the results of these tests.

- The diversity of our big country makes the tests difficult to determine the norm.
- Students that are talented in areas other than math and language cannot show their talent.
- Students who do not speak and read English fluently will not perform well on standardized tests.
- Students who live in poverty do not necessarily have the experiences necessary to comprehend the questions.

The list could go on, but there does have to be some sort of assessment of progress that a community can use to decide how their schools are doing. Standardized tests and their results are receiving more and more attention these days. The purpose of this series, along with creating better readers, is to help students get better results on standardized tests.

Test Success

The ability to do well when taking traditional standardized tests on comprehension requires at least three things:

- a large vocabulary of sight words
- the mastery of certain specific test-taking skills
- the ability to recognize and control stress

Vocabulary has already been discussed in detail. Test-taking skills and recognizing and controlling stress are techniques that can be taught and will be discussed in this section.

Introduction (cont.)

Test-Taking Skills

Every student in your class needs good test-taking skills, and almost all of them will need to be taught these skills. Even fluent readers and extremely logical students will fair better on standardized tests if they are taught a few simple skills for taking tests.

These test-taking skills are:

- The ability to follow complicated and sometimes confusing directions. Teach students to break down the directions and translate them into easy, understandable words. Use this series to teach them the types of questions that will appear.

- The ability to scale back what they know and concentrate on just what is asked and what is contained in the text—show them how to restrict their responses. Question students on their answers when doing practice exercises and have them show where they found the answer in the text.

- The ability to rule out confusing distracters in multiple choice answers. Teach students to look for key words and match up the information from the text.

- The ability to maintain concentration during boring and tedious repetition. Use practice time to practice this and reward students for maintaining concentration. Explain to students why they are practicing and why their concentration is important for the day of the test.

There are also environmental elements that you can practice with throughout the year in order for your students to become more accustomed to them for the testing period.

If your desks are pushed together, have students move them apart so they will be accustomed to the feel on test-taking day.

- Put a "Testing—Do Not Disturb" sign on the door.
- Require "test etiquette" when practicing: no talking, attentive listening, and following directions.
- Provide a strip of construction paper for each student to use as a marker.
- Establish a routine for replacing broken pencils. Give each student two sharpened pencils and have a back-up supply ready. Tell students they will need to raise their broken pencil in their hand, and you will give them a new one. One thing students should not worry about is the teacher's reaction to a broken pencil.
- Read the instructions to the students as you would when giving a standardized test so they grow accustomed to your test-giving voice.
- As a teacher, you probably realize that what is practiced daily is what is best learned. All of these practices work well to help students improve their scores.

Introduction (cont.)

Reduce Stress and Build Confidence

As well as the physical and mental aspects of test-taking, there is also the psychological. It is important to reduce students' stress and increase students' confidence during the year.

- In order to reduce stress, it first needs to be recognized. Discuss feelings and apprehensions about testing. Give students some tools for handling stress.

- Begin talking about good habits at the beginning of the year. Talk about getting enough sleep, eating a good breakfast, and exercising before and after school. Consider sending home a letter encouraging parents to start these good routines with their children at home.

- Explain the power of positive thought to your students. Tell them to use their imaginations to visualize themselves doing well. Let them know that they have practiced all year and are ready for what is to come.

- Remember to let students stretch and walk around between tests. Try using "Simon Says" with younger students throughout the year to get them to breathe deeply, stretch, and relax so it won't be a novel idea during test time.

- Build confidence during the year when using the practice tests. Emphasize that these tests are for learning. If they could get all of the answers right the first time, they wouldn't need any practice. Encourage students to state at least one thing they learned from doing the practice test.

- Give credit for reasonable answers. Explain to students that the test makers write answers that seem almost true to really test the students' understanding. Encourage students to explain why they chose the answers they gave, and then reason with the whole class on how not to be duped the next time.

- Promote a relaxed, positive outlook on test-taking. Let your students know on the real day that they are fully prepared to do their best.

Introduction (cont.)

Suggestions for the Teacher

When practicing skills for comprehension, it is important to vocalize and discuss the process in finding an answer. After building vocabulary, tapping background knowledge, and discussing the structure that might be used in the article, have the students read the article. If they are not able to read the article independently, have them read with a partner or in a small teacher-led group. After completing these steps, work through the comprehension questions. The following are suggestions for working through these activities.

- Have students read the text silently and answer the questions.

- Have students correct their own papers.

- Discuss each answer and how the students came to their answers.

- Refer to the exact wording in the text.

- Discuss whether students had to tap their own knowledge or not.

Answer Sheet

The teacher can choose to use the blank answer sheet located at the back of the book for practice filling in bubble forms for standardized tests. The rows have not been numbered so that the teacher can use the form for any test, filling in the numbers and copying for the class as necessary. The teacher can also have the students write the answers directly on the pages of the test practice sheets instead of using the bubble sheet.

CD-ROM

A CD-ROM with all the lessons, answer sheet, and answer key has been provided at the back of this book.

Summary

Teachers need to find a way to blend test preparation with the process of learning and discovery. It is important for students to learn test-taking skills and strategies because they will be important throughout life. It is more important for students to build vocabulary and knowledge, to create frameworks for comprehension, and to become fluent readers.

The *Nonfiction Comprehension Test Practice* series is an outstanding program to start your students in the direction of becoming better readers and test-takers. These are skills they will need throughout life. Provide an atmosphere of the joy of learning and create a climate for curiosity within your classroom. With daily practice of comprehension skills and test-taking procedures, teaching comprehension may seem just a little bit easier.

Level 4   Lesson 1

Name_____   Date_____

Sentence Comprehension

Directions: Read the following sentence carefully and answer the questions below "True" (T) or "False" (F).

> The other kids started to scream, but Larry ran up to the front and stopped the bus.

1. Larry and all the kids started screaming. _____
2. Larry wasn't able to stop the bus. _____
3. Larry was in the front and ran to the back to stop the bus. _____
4. Larry was in a hurry to stop the bus. _____
5. A group of kids were in a bus. _____

Word Study

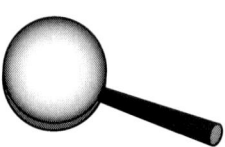

Directions: Read the definition below and match the words in Column A with the words in Column B to form a hyphenated word. The first one has been done for you.

hyphen
The article begins, "Talk about a real-life hero! Ten-year-old Larry Champagne III...." In the article, the words *real-life* and *ten-year-old* are combined with hyphens. A **hyphen** is a punctuation mark used to join words and numbers.

Column A	Column B
all	ray
dot	year-old
Fourteen	purpose
X	matrix
T	rated
PG	bone

Word with Hyphen

1. *all-purpose*
2. _____
3. _____
4. _____
5. _____
6. _____

©Shell Educational Publishing   #10334 Nonfiction Comprehension Test Practice   21

Paragraph Comprehension

Directions: Read the paragraph below and answer the following questions.

> Larry's speedy reaction made the news all over the country. He appeared on TV shows as a hero. The bus company gave Larry a $100 gift certificate to spend at a local toy store. His school hung a medal of honor around his neck.

1. Larry was honored for his
   a. quick action as a hero.
   b. work at a local toy store.
   c. bravery against the school bully.
   d. kindness to the students in his class.

2. Larry received from his school
   a. an invitation to a talk show.
   b. a $100 gift certificate to a local toy store.
   c. a medal of honor.
   d. a certificate for his bravery.

3. A gift certificate is a
   a. check.
   b. bill.
   c. coupon.
   d. credit to spend at a store.

4. What made news all over the country?
   a. the bus accident
   b. Larry's speedy reaction to save the bus
   c. the $100 gift certificate to a local toy store
   d. the medal of honor around Larry's neck

5. Who gave the gift certificate to Larry?
   a. Larry's school
   b. the bus company
   c. the TV shows
   d. the news organizations

Whole-Story Comprehension

Directions: Read the story below and answer the questions on the following page.

A Lucky Brake

Talk about a real-life hero! Ten-year-old Larry Champagne III from St. Louis, Missouri, hit the brakes on a runaway school bus. He saved himself and 20 other kids on board from disaster.

It all happened in one big scary flash. On the way to school, the bus driver, Ernestine Blackman, suddenly blacked out and slumped over the steering wheel. The bus started swaying, banging into the guardrails. The other kids started to scream, but Larry ran to the front and stopped the bus.

"At first I thought, 'We're gonna die,'" says Larry, "but after I pressed the brake, I felt safe."

Larry's speedy reaction made news all over the country. He appeared on TV shows as a hero. The bus company gave Larry a $100 gift certificate to spend at a local toy store. His school hung a medal of honor around his neck.

"My grandmother always tells me to do what's right," says Larry. He gives credit to his brother, Jerrick, 9, who "helped me get the bus driver up" during the emergency. Now the driver, who had a circulation problem called a stroke, is recovering.

How did he know how to stop the bus? Larry is something of a mechanic. He helps his grandfather work on his old truck. "He gets his hands dirty," says his grandfather. One thing is certain: Larry knows where to find the brakes.

Level 4　　　　　　　　　　　　　　　　　　　　　　　　　　　　　　　　　　　　Lesson 1

Name_____　Date_____

Whole-Story Comprehension (cont.)

Directions: After you have finished the story on the previous page, answer the questions below.

1. What did Larry do to save the runaway bus?

   a. He parked it for the sleeping bus driver.
   b. He slammed on the brakes.
   c. He dialed 911.
   d. He helped all the kids climb out through the window.

2. Who taught Larry to do what's right?

   a. his mother
   b. his father
   c. his grandmother
   d. his uncle

3. How did Larry know how to stop the bus?

   a. He watched a show on TV about buses.
   b. He read the driver's manual.
   c. He works on an old truck with his grandfather.
   d. The bus driver had shown him how.

4. What do Larry and his grandfather work on?

   a. They work on an old tractor.
   b. They work on homework together.
   c. They work on an old truck.
   d. They work on model airplanes.

5. When did Larry finally feel safe?

   a. once he pressed the brake, and the bus stopped
   b. when the police officers showed up
   c. when the kids finally stopped screaming
   d. when the bus driver started driving again

6. A stroke is

   a. when a person has a circulation problem.
   b. when a person is in jail.
   c. when a person slams on the brakes.
   d. when a person has a heart attack.

7. Larry gives credit to his brother, Jerrick, for

   a. teaching him how to stop the bus.
   b. helping him work on his old truck.
   c. teaching him CPR.
   d. helping him get the bus driver up.

8. In which order did the events occur?

   a. Ms. Blackman blacked out and slumped over the steering wheel, the bus started swaying, banging into the guardrails, and the kids began screaming.
   b. The bus started swaying and banging into the guardrails, the kids began screaming, Ms. Blackman blacked out, and slumped over the steering wheel.
   c. Ms. Blackman slumped over the steering wheel and blacked out, the bus started banging into the guardrails and swaying, the kids started screaming.
   d. The kids started screaming, Ms. Blackman blacked out and slumped over the steering wheel, the bus began bumping into the guardrails, and then the bus began swaying.

Enrichment

Directions: Read the information below and use it to find the correct definitions.

What is a *stroke*? The word *stroke* can be a verb or a noun and has many definitions. Read the different dictionary definitions of the word *stroke* in Group A and match them to the sentences in Group B. Write the letter that corresponds to each definition next to the sentences.

Group A

A. (v) to rub gently in one direction

B. (v) to flatter or pay attention with the intent to persuade

C. (n) a controlled swing, intending to hit a ball

D. (n) an unexpected result

E. (n) loss of consciousness and/or sensation caused by rupture or obstruction of an artery in the brain

F. (n) energetic or vigorous effort

G. (n) the sound of a bell being struck

Group B

_____ 1. At the *stroke* of twelve, the New Year began.

_____ 2. She tried to *stroke* his ego, but it didn't seem to help.

_____ 3. With the *stroke* of his club, the ball sailed off the golf course.

_____ 4. She suffered a *stroke* last Christmas.

_____ 5. With a *stroke* of luck, she managed to win the contest.

_____ 6. He *stroked* the newborn puppy with his finger.

_____ 7. With a *stroke* of genius, she reinvented the process.

Level 4   Lesson 1

Name_____ Date_____

Graphic Development

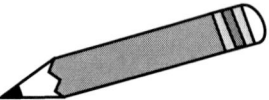

Directions: You have just read about a bus accident that occurred because the bus driver, Ms. Blackman, suffered a stroke. A stroke can affect emotions, movement, understanding, speech, touching, moving, and thinking. A stroke is when the circulation of blood in an artery to the brain has become blocked or bursts. Use the diagram of the human brain below to answer the questions. Read the effects of a stroke and fill in the part or parts of the brain that would most likely be affected because of the stroke. The first one has been done for you.

Part(s) of the Brain Affected   **Effects of Having a Stroke**

__Arm Control__   **1.** Mobility and feeling in the right arm is lost.

_____   **2.** A person has trouble reading and seeing things clearly.

_____   **3.** One side of the face can become paralyzed and unable to move after a stroke.

_____   **4.** Objects may look closer or farther away than they really are, causing spills or collisions when walking.

_____   **5.** Muscles used in talking can be affected which causes speech to be slurred, slowed, or distorted.

_____   **6.** Hearing isn't usually affected, but speech can be hard to understand.

_____   **7.** The ability to walk or put weight on one leg is lost.

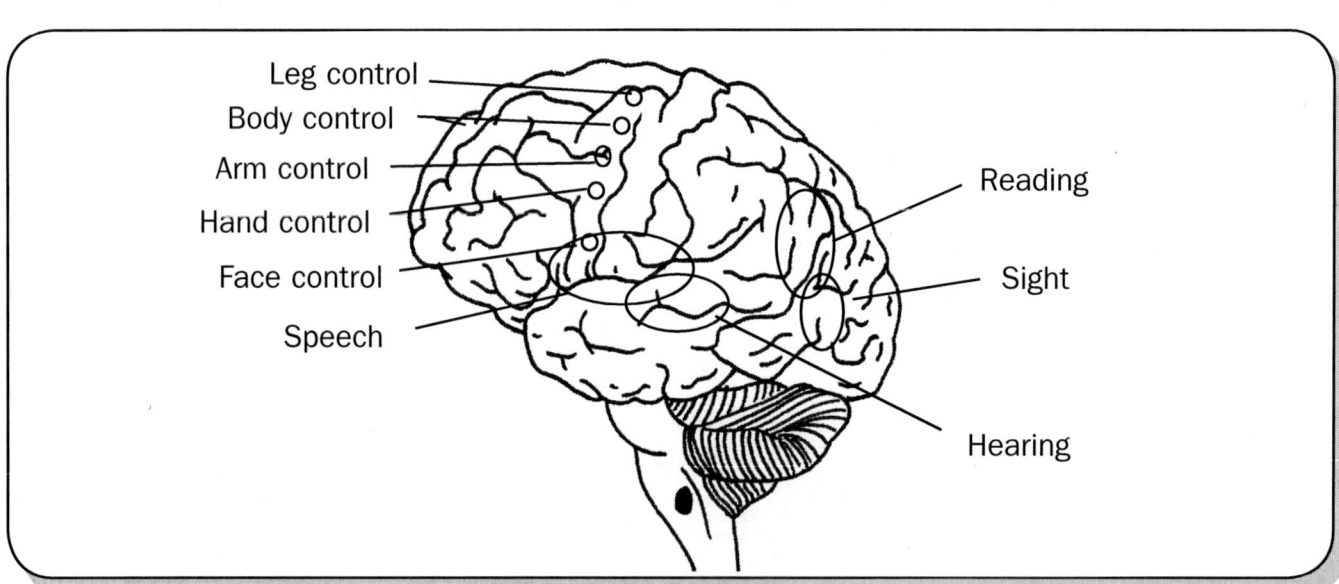

26   #10334 Nonfiction Comprehension Test Practice   ©Shell Educational Publishing

Sentence Comprehension

Directions: Read the following sentence carefully and answer the questions below "True" (T) or "False" (F).

> As I wondered what to do, a strange new noise began to float out of our drawer.

1. The author of the article knows what to do in this situation. _____
2. The author knows what is inside the drawer. _____
3. The author was trying to figure out what to do. _____
4. The noise was floating out of the cupboard. _____
5. The noise was old and familiar. _____

Word Study

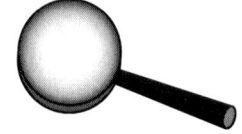

Directions: Look at the examples of personification, and then write other forms of personification using the objects below.

float

The word *float* means to continue to drift or change position. The word *float* comes from the Middle English word *flote*, which means *boat*. In the article, the word *float* is used to mean drift. " . . . a strange new noise began to float out of the drawer." The noise began to float or drift. The noise seems to be taking on the characteristics of a person. This is called *personification*. Personification is a figure of speech in which an animal, an object, or an idea is given the characteristics of a person.

The book flipped open.

The tree branches reached high into the sky.

The shack stood firm against the storm.

house _____

wind _____

leaves _____

cloud _____

Paragraph Comprehension

Directions: Read the paragraph below and answer the following questions.

> My brain was racing. Spots must have slipped into the bottom cupboard last night when I reached in for a pan. We had noticed she loved nothing better than getting into "caves." A file drawer or box or laundry tub would do. A cupboard was good.

1. What did Spots like getting into?
    a. She liked getting into trouble.
    b. She liked getting into containers like "caves."
    c. She liked getting into the car without anyone noticing.
    d. She liked getting into the cat food.

2. When does the author think that Spots slipped into the bottom cupboard?
    a. after breakfast
    b. when they were installing the cupboards
    c. when the author reached in for a pan
    d. after the mail was delivered

3. What does the phrase, "my brain was racing" mean?
    a. my brain is in a race with another brain
    b. my brain is like a car
    c. my brain stopped working
    d. my brain is thinking quickly

4. Why did Spots slip into the cupboard?
    a. She wanted to play with the other cats.
    b. She was hoping to find her owner.
    c. That's where her food was kept.
    d. She liked to climb inside of things.

5. What does the word "slipped" mean in this paragraph?
    a. fell over
    b. jumped over
    c. sneaked into
    d. opened

Whole-Story Comprehension

Directions: Read the story below and answer the questions on the following page.

A Sticky Situation

When I walked into the kitchen, I knew something was wrong. There was an odd rustling noise. It sounded like a critter quietly pushing objects around. A mouse! A mouse in the house! Where was Spots?

Weeks earlier, we had adopted this half-grown, hungry cat we found in the yard. She was white with gray splotches and a bushy gray tail as big around as her body. She was long and lean like a dancer. She could wind her body in and out of the stairway spindles as though she had a snake's spine. She had the hungry look and in-your-face attitude of a tough street cat. Sending a mouse packing, I thought, ought to be just her speed.

But just now she was nowhere to be seen. I heard the rustling again. Something with four paws was rifling through my belongings. I'd have to track down the trespasser alone.

The noises drew me even closer to the utensil drawer. It was a tangle of measuring cups and spoons, knives, pizza cutters, can openers, and much more. O.K. The mouse must be in there.

As I wondered what to do, a strange new noise began to float out of the drawer. It was a happy, low motor noise you can't mistake for anything else. It was a purr!

My brain was racing. Spots must have slipped into the bottom cupboard last night when I reached in for a pan. We had noticed she loved nothing better than getting into "caves." A file drawer or box or laundry tub would do. A cupboard was good.

I must have shut the door, closing her inside her new cave. Then the explorer must have leaped up and into the drawer from the back. This was heaven! The smallest cave yet.

I tried the drawer. It slid out an inch or two. The cat was wedged in there, tight! I could make out a pink nose and glowing eyes, but I couldn't open the drawer. At least, not without removing her coat. She meowed a friendly greeting and kept purring. She wasn't worried, but I was. I could barely poke my fingers into the drawer. How was I going to unstick the cat?

Eureka! I had it! I started removing utensils one by one from the front. Bit by bit, the drawer became a roomier place. Slowly, it became free enough to slide out another inch, then another. At last, out stepped one snaky, white and gray cat, looking quite pleased with herself. She stretched and sauntered away, without a care in the world. I swear, she was grinning.

Whole-Story Comprehension (cont.)

Directions: After you have read the story on the previous page, answer the questions below.

1. Who does the word "I" refer to in this article?
   a. the cat
   b. the author of the article
   c. the publisher
   d. the bus driver

2. What did Spots like getting into?
   a. caves
   b. messes
   c. trouble
   d. the pool

3. If the drawer was opened with Spots still inside, what might happen?
   a. She would be happy.
   b. Her coat might be removed.
   c. She would be able to eat better.
   d. She would purr.

4. How did they get Spots, the cat?
   a. She was a kitten from their previous cat.
   b. They found her in the yard.
   c. They adopted her a year ago.
   d. They got her from the neighbors.

5. At first, what did the author think was making the noise?
   a. a mouse
   b. a dog
   c. a kitten
   d. a snake

6. What sound was coming from the drawer?
   a. a growl
   b. a purr
   c. a creaking sound
   d. a squeak

7. How did the cat get into the drawer?
   a. She was pushed inside.
   b. When the author reached in for a pan, she must have slipped in.
   c. She jumped in.
   d. none of the above

8. What does the author think the cat was doing at the end of the article?
   a. scratching
   b. howling
   c. screeching
   d. grinning

Name_____ Date_____

Enrichment

Directions: Read the information in the box below. Then read the sentences and determine which type of context clue you would use to determine the definition of the italicized word. Write the type of context clue you would use on each line.

> **She stretched and *sauntered* away without a care in the world.**
>
> What does the word *sauntered* mean? One way to determine the definition of a word is to look it up in the dictionary. Another way to figure out a definition is to use context clues in the sentence.
>
> Each time you write a sentence, the words in the sentence depend upon each other to make sense. The words in a sentence put each other in context. There are different types of context clues. Read the types of context clues and examples of each below.
>
> **Synonyms**—This is when a word is written with another word with a similar meaning.
>
> Example: He was disgusted, *frustrated*, and annoyed with the student.
>
> **Association**—Given enough information, one can determine the definition of a word.
>
> Example: Brian didn't do very well in school. Each time he got his report card, his grades in reading and writing were failing grades. His teachers didn't see much progress in language arts. The boy was *illiterate*.
>
> **Series**—Clues to the definition of a word can be found when a word is surrounded by other similar items in a series.
>
> Example: The *oboe*, clarinet, and bassoon are all very similar instruments.
>
> **Tone and Setting**—The tone and setting can give clues to the meaning of a word.
>
> Example: As the alarm went off, the *frightened* child was shoved, pushed, and forced to leave the classroom.
>
> **Cause and Effect**—A cause and effect relationship can indicate the meaning of a word.
>
> Example: Since all of the students *failed* the test, they will have to take the test over again.

1. The clouds came rolling in quickly. The streets were *eerily* quiet and it was very spooky.

_____

2. Since Sam *trained* everyday, he won the race.

_____

3. The warm welcome, *hospitality*, and good cheer made the guests feel at home.

_____

4. The dirt started crumbling away on the hill, and the path has worn away. It is not safe to walk in the area. The land has started to *erode*.

_____

5. She was happy, *exhilarated*, and cheerful with the outcome.

_____

Level 4　　　　　　　　　　　　　　　　　　　　　　　　　　　　　　　　Lesson 2

Name_____ Date_____

Graphic Development

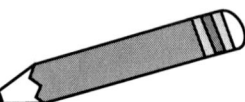

Directions: Use the sequence map below to answer the questions that follow.

Title
Sticky Situation

1. Author walks into kitchen and hears noise.

2. The cat is described.

4. The author hears a purr!

3. The noises draw the author to a utensil drawer.

5. The author sees a pink nose and glowing eyes.

6. The author removes utensils one by one to free the cat.

Concluding Summary or Statement
The author sees the cat grin.

1. What happens first in the article? _____

2. Who are the characters in this article? _____

3. Did the author hear the noise or see the cat first? _____

4. What is the last thing that happened in the article? _____

5. What happened after the author discovered the cat was in the drawer? _____

32　#10334 Nonfiction Comprehension Test Practice　　　　　©Shell Educational Publishing

Level 4

Lesson 3

Name_____ Date_____

Sentence Comprehension

Directions: Read the following sentence carefully and answer the questions below "True" (T) or "False" (F).

> I found myself out on the dark January streets, jumping over snow banks and skidding along icy patches of sidewalk.

1. It was dark when the author ran. _____
2. There were snow banks and icy patches along the sidewalks. _____
3. The author is guaranteed a medal at the marathon. _____
4. The author was running during the winter. _____
5. The sidewalk had been scraped by the snow plow, so the run was easier. _____

Word Study

Directions: Write the words for the sounds below.

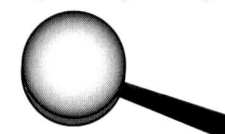

> **bang!**
> The definition of *bang* is a sudden loud noise. The word *bang* is also a form of onomatopoeia. Onomatopoeia is a word that sounds like its meaning. Examples of onomatopoeia are buzz, gunk, swish, zing, or zip!

1. the sound of your heart beating _____

2. the sound of boots in the snow _____

3. the sound of soda in a cup of ice _____

4. the sound of a snake _____

5. the sound of a clock _____

6. the sound of being hit by something _____

Name_____ Date_____

Paragraph Comprehension

Directions: Read the paragraph below and answer the following questions.

> There were times when I regretted the dare. I had never run more than eight miles at a stretch before, and here I was training for over three times that distance. To make matters worse, since the race was in April, I had to run throughout the winter and, in Boston, winters are cold. For most people just putting on their shirts, sweaters, jackets, mittens, and hats is exercise enough. I found myself out on the dark January streets, jumping over snow banks and skidding along icy patches of sidewalk. Even in gloves, my fingers got so cold that they felt like rolls of pennies; my nose didn't defrost until lunchtime!

1. How does the author feel about running in the Boston Marathon?

   a. The author thinks that it is a great idea.
   b. The author feels like it is something that must be done.
   c. The author, at times, regretted the dare to run in the race.
   d. The author can't wait to run the race in the cold weather.

2. What were some of the trials the author had to overcome to run in the race?

   a. The author needed physical therapy treatments to run.
   b. The author had to wait until the cast was off.
   c. The author had to train in the freezing winter and had to run more miles at one time than ever before.
   d. The author needed to learn how to run in order to race.

3. Up to how many miles did the author run before training for the marathon?

   a. 8 miles
   b. 10 miles
   c. 5 miles more than ever before
   d. around 24 miles

4. Which sentence best describes how the author felt about the gloves?

   a. The gloves made the cold manageable.
   b. The gloves were necessary to keep warm.
   c. The gloves were too big and kept falling off.
   d. The gloves weren't warm enough to keep the fingers from feeling like rolls of pennies.

5. Why did the author have to train in the winter?

   a. It was easier to train in the winter.
   b. Because the race was in April.
   c. It was too hot to race in the summer.
   d. The race officials felt like the winter would be the best season to train.

Whole Story Comprehension

Directions: Read the story below and answer the questions on the following page.

Marathon Madness

What makes 15,000 men and women take off their jackets on a chilly day in April and run for four hours or more through the streets of greater Boston? Put like that, it certainly sounds silly, but I was one of those runners. In fact, like everybody else, I even paid for the experience. The race is called the Boston Marathon, and people have been competing in it since 1897.

"I could do that," I said.

"No, you couldn't," my friend Ed replied.

"Want to bet?" I said. That's how it happened.

There were times when I regretted the dare. I had never run more than eight miles at a stretch before, and here I was training for over three times that distance. To make matters worse, since the race was in April, I had to run throughout the winter, and in Boston, winters are cold. For most people, just putting on their shirts, sweaters, jackets, mittens, and hats is exercise enough. I found myself out on the dark January streets, jumping over snow banks and skidding along icy patches of sidewalk. Even in gloves, my fingers got so cold that they felt like rolls of pennies; my nose didn't defrost until lunchtime!

Finally, the big day arrived. The weather was cold, with ice and rain. Bang! The gun sounded, and we were off. Well, I didn't actually go anywhere at first because I was standing behind so many people I had to wait for them to move. It was like being in a traffic jam, so I jumped up and down to stay warm.

At first, the running was easy. The other runners just seemed to pull me along. Somewhere around the 20-mile mark I even caught myself thinking, "This is nothing. Why did I train so hard?"

That's when I hit "the wall." I didn't actually run into a brick wall, but it felt as if I had. "The wall" is what marathoners call the point at which your body simply runs out of gas. My legs turned to rubber; my arms turned into pieces of wood. I thought I might pass out. I can't remember anything about the last five miles of the race.

I kept running though. At least, that's what Ed told me at the finish line.

"You looked good," he said. "How did it feel?"

"Terrific," I lied. I wasn't going to let him get the last laugh.

Level 4   Lesson 3

Name_____ Date_____

Whole Story Comprehension (cont.)

Directions: After you have read the story on the previous page, answer the questions below.

1. Which marathon did the author run in?
   a. Boston Marathon
   b. New York Marathon
   c. Chicago Marathon
   d. United States Marathon

2. Which sentence best describes the weather on race day?
   a. sunny, with a cool breeze
   b. cold, with ice and rain
   c. cold, with snow and hail
   d. cold, with rain and snow

3. What felt like rolls of pennies to the author?
   a. his feet
   b. his toes
   c. his arms
   d. his fingers

4. Based on the article, what might someone do to prepare for a marathon?
   a. One must be willing to train many hours and put in a lot of miles.
   b. One must eat certain foods and get plenty of sleep.
   c. One must be an experienced runner to train for the marathon.
   d. One must be willing to eat, sleep, and train twenty-four hours a day.

5. Why do you think the author couldn't remember anything about the last five miles of the race?
   a. The author was knocked out and couldn't remember the rest of the race.
   b. The author was blindfolded and led along the last five miles.
   c. The author was so exhausted that he couldn't remember the last five miles.
   d. The author was hit by a car in the race and was carried by ambulance to the hospital.

6. What does it mean to hit "the wall"?
   a. Your body hits a brick wall and you have injuries.
   b. Your body reaches a point where it can't go anymore.
   c. Your body becomes paralyzed and you can't move your arms and legs.
   d. Your mind reaches a point where it stops functioning and you can't continue.

7. In this article, to whom does "I" refer?
   a. the winner of the Boston Marathon
   b. the friend
   c. the person who came in last place
   d. the author of the article and the person who ran in the marathon

8. Why did the author lie about how he felt while running the race?
   a. The author would be disqualified if officials found out the truth.
   b. The author wasn't willing to accept the truth.
   c. The author wanted his friend to think he wasn't feeling well.
   d. The author didn't want his friend to laugh at him.

Enrichment

Directions: Read the information below and use it to find the similes in the sentences below. Write the similes on the lines following the sentences.

Making Comparisons

By comparing something to something else, a writer is able to help the reader see more clearly what is being described. Comparisons that use the words *like* or *as* are called **similes**. An example of a simile used in the article is, "My fingers felt like rolls of pennies."

A simile can be used to:

- create a visual image
- describe an object that is unknown
- set the mood for a piece of writing
- describe characters and settings

Examples of Similes:

As	Like
quick as a bunny	fall like rain
sharp as a tack	twisted like a pretzel
fit as a fiddle	fly like a butterfly
blind as a bat	crush it like grapes
straight as an arrow	sleep like a cat
thin as a rail	shoot up like oil

---

1. At the end of the race I had legs like rubber.

Simile: _____

2. Not many people can walk like chickens.

Simile: _____

3. At the 20-mile mark, she had hands like pieces of wood.

Simile: _____

4. She was as fast as a steam locomotive.

Simile: _____

Graphic Development

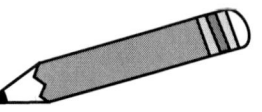

Directions: Read the following information and use the bar graph below to answer the questions.

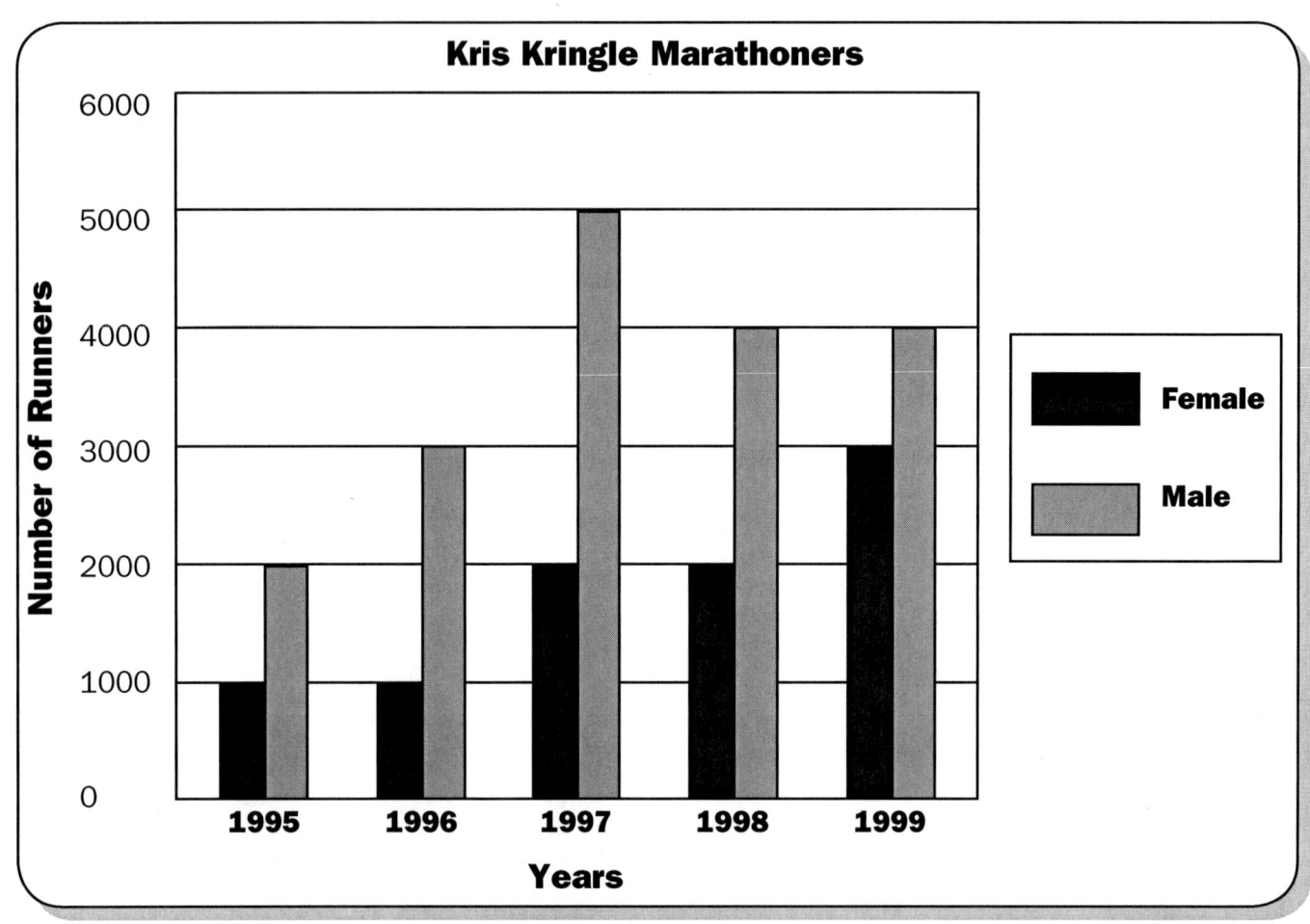

Kris Kringle Marathoners

(Bar graph showing Number of Runners by Year, 1995–1999, for Female and Male)

- 1995: Female 1000, Male 2000
- 1996: Female 1000, Male 3000
- 1997: Female 2000, Male 5000
- 1998: Female 2000, Male 4000
- 1999: Female 3000, Male 4000

More and more people are taking up the challenge of running a marathon. Running a marathon requires sacrifice, determination, and endurance. Many long hours of training are necessary to be able to complete a marathon.

1. What is the total number of runners in the Kris Kringle Marathon in 1995?

2. Do more male or female runners run in the Kris Kringle Marathon?

3. How many more male runners than female runners ran in 1998?

4. What do you notice about the number of male runners in 1997 compared to 1999?

5. What is the total number of female runners that have participated in the Kris Kringle Marathon between 1995 and 1999?

Level 4 Lesson 4

Name_____ Date_____

Sentence Comprehension

Directions: Read the following sentence carefully and answer the questions below "True" (T) or "False" (F).

> Michelle Roehm, editor of *Girls Know Best,* says the book "encourages girls to speak out and be heard."

1. The book, *Girls Know Best,* is a fictional book. _____
2. People reading this book will find information on what girls think. _____
3. This book is written especially for girls. _____
4. *Girls Know Best* is the title of the book. _____
5. The book allows an opportunity for boys to talk to each other. _____

Word Study

Directions: Read the information in the box and use the words listed below to complete the sentences.

> **camaraderie**
>
> The definition of *camaraderie* is a spirit of friendly, good-fellowship. Camaraderie comes from the French word *comrade*, meaning companion. Many of the words we use come from different languages.

croissants   commode   rodeo   mustang   lariat

1. _____ comes from the Spanish word *rodear*, which means to surround.

2. _____ comes from the French word *commodus*, meaning suitable or convenient.

3. _____ comes from the Spanish word *la riata*, meaning rope.

4. _____ comes from the Spanish word *musteno*, meaning stray.

5. _____ comes from the Middle French word *creissant*, meaning flaky roll.

Level 4   Lesson 4

Name_____ Date_____

Paragraph Comprehension

Directions: Read the paragraph below and answer the following questions.

> Have you ever laughed so hard that it made you snort? Forgotten to zip up your pants all the way? Zoya Ahmadi, 14, feels your pain. Says Zoya: "I know being embarrassed in public is one of the worst things girls have to face." But rather than bury her face after slipups like those, Zoya wrote a chapter of advice to help other girls avoid embarrassing moments.

1. According to this paragraph, what is one of the worst things girls have to face?
    a. laughing so hard you snort
    b. forgetting to zip up your pants all the way
    c. being embarrassed in public
    d. tripping and falling down

2. Who is Zoya Ahmadi?
    a. Zoya is the editor of the book, *Girls Know Best*.
    b. Zoya wrote one of the chapters in the book, *Girls Know Best*.
    c. Zoya wrote the entire book, *Girls Know Best*.
    d. Zoya is a girl who likes to use big words in her reports.

3. What is the meaning of the word *slipup*?
    a. A slipup is when you mess up and do something embarrassing.
    b. A slipup is something you wear under your dress.
    c. A slipup is when you call your friend to come play.
    d. A slipup is a presentation of a report you have studied.

4. What are some examples in this paragraph of things that might be embarrassing?
    a. eating with your mouth full
    b. dialing the wrong number on the phone
    c. getting tongue-tied and forgetting what you wanted to say
    d. laughing so hard you snort or forgetting to zip your pants all the way

5. The chapter written by Zoya is meant to
    a. teach girls the best way to make friends.
    b. help girls learn to speak in public.
    c. help girls avoid embarrassing moments.
    d. help girls avoid meeting new people.

Lesson 4

ARTICLE FROM TIME FOR KIDS

Name_____ Date_____

Whole-Story Comprehension

Directions: Read the story below and answer the questions on the following page.

Do Girls Know Best?

Have you ever laughed so hard that it made you snort? Forgotten to zip up your pants all the way? Zoya Ahmadi, 14, feels your pain. Says Zoya: "I know being embarrassed in public is one of the worst things girls have to face." But rather than bury her face after slipups like those, Zoya wrote a chapter of advice to help other girls avoid embarrassing moments.

Zoya's chapter is one of 26 in a new book called *Girls Know Best*. All the chapters were written by girls, ages 7 to 16, and chosen through a national writing contest. Michelle Roehm, editor of *Girls Know Best,* says the book "encourages girls to speak out and be heard. It's a way for them to talk to each other."

Girls across the country had a lot to say. Sisters Rebecca and Melissa Rushing, 13 and 7, sounded off about surviving sibling battles. Friends Kyra Borg and Katie Arnold, both 13, co-wrote a chapter called "BIG Words to Use to Impress Friends, Parents, and Teachers." "Kyra and I like using big words because they help on reports," says Katie. "And it's fun to use them on each other."

The book's 38 young authors have visited stores around the country and autographed hundreds of books—mostly for girls. "This book kind of gets a camaraderie going among us girls," says Kyra. "Sometimes girls are afraid to speak up, compared to boys."

Another *Girls Know Best* book is already in the works. Also, for boys who think they know best, your turn is coming: a boys-only book is on the way.

In addition to *Girls Know Best*, you can find in *Girls Know Best 2* advice on shyness, the Internet, making money, and slumber parties. The authors are 47 girls, ages 7 to 15, from all over the country. They won the Girl Writer Contest sponsored by the publishers, Beyond Words Publishing, Inc.

Girls Know Best 3 consists of "real-life advice" from 30 girls from across the U.S. and Canada. Topics covered include tips on how to start your own rock band, great games for the car, and discovering your family's history.

Because the *Girls* books have been so popular, the publishers decided to share the "wise thoughts and wacky ideas from guys like you" in *Boys Know It All*. Thirty-two "cool guys," ages 7 to 16, give advice about—of all things—dealing with girls. Other topics are making comic strips and "great guy grub."

If you would like your ideas published, you might read the "Do You Want to Be a Published Author?" section in *Girls Know Best 3*—and enter either a *Girls Know Best* or a *Boys Know It All* contest. Follow the advice of Phillip and Andrew, 12-year-old authors in the *Boys* book: "Hey Guys! Don't be afraid to try something new. Have a little fun. Be creative. Dream."

Whole-Story Comprehension (cont.)

Directions: After you have read the story on the previous page, answer the questions below.

1. What is the book, *Girls Know Best*, about?
   a. a book about a group of girls that have been friends forever
   b. a book about learning friendship skills
   c. a book that offers advice by girls for girls
   d. a book that offers words of encouragement for new kids

2. Who wrote the chapters in the book?
   a. a group of peers, ages 6 to 18
   b. a group of teachers
   c. a group of girls, ages 7 to 16
   d. a female publisher

3. How were the authors chosen?
   a. authors were elected to write a chapter
   b. authors were selected through a national writing contest
   c. authors were handpicked by the editor of the book
   d. authors submitted their work to a publisher

4. The targeted audience for the book is
   a. girls.
   b. boys.
   c. teachers.
   d. mothers.

5. What were some of the subjects addressed in the book?
   a. avoiding embarrassing moments, surviving sibling battles, and words to impress friends
   b. making new friends and learning to cook
   c. study habits and learning to write book reports
   d. changing your attitude about life and doing better in school

6. How are the authors publicizing the book?
   a. They are touring the country visiting hundreds of middle and high schools.
   b. They are sending a variety of letters to young girls throughout the country.
   c. They are visiting hundreds of stores around the country.
   d. They are filming a music video.

7. How did the authors in *Girls Know Best 2* get their articles published?
   a. They were good friends with the editor.
   b. They won a writing contest.
   c. They met the daughter of the publisher on a plane.
   d. They each paid the publisher $50.

8. What topics are included in *Boys Know It All*?
   a. girls, grub, guys
   b. comics, girls, slumber parties
   c. girls, grub, comics
   d. games, girls, grub

Enrichment

Directions: Read the following information and use it to answer the questions below.

> It is important to remember how to punctuate and capitalize the titles of books, movies, and magazines in your writing. In the article, "Girls Know Best," the book title is italicized each time. Read the rules for how to punctuate and capitalize titles in writing.
>
> Capitalize the first word of a title, the last word, and every word in between except for short words like conjunctions and words such as *a*, *an*, and *the*.
>
> **Examples:**
> *The Adventures of Tom Sawyer* (book/movie)
> *Girls Know Best* (book)
> *Better Homes and Gardens* (magazine)
> *The Civil War* (book)
>
> Punctuate a title of a magazine, newspaper, movie, book, and play the same way. They are all put in italics on the computer. If you are doing your work in your own handwriting, then you need to underline the titles instead of italicizing them.
>
> **Examples:**
> He is the editor for the *Las Vegas Tribune*. (newspaper)
> *Les Miserables* is a musical on Broadway. (play/musical)
> The first play I ever saw was *Death of a Salesman*. (play)
>
> Use quotations to punctuate the title of a song, a chapter in a book, a one-act play, or an article found in a newspaper or magazine.
>
> **Examples:**
> "I Love the Way You Love Me" (song)
> "The Outer Space" (article in magazine)

Rewrite the sentences capitalizing and punctuating the titles, as necessary.

1. I hope that I can get tickets to phantom of the opera. _____

2. The name of the movie showing right now is return of the jedi. _____

3. My favorite song right now is out of my dreams, by Jo Mack. _____

4. Better homes and gardens has some good tips on housecleaning. _____

5. Where did you put today's issue of the chicago tribune? _____

Graphic Development

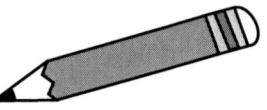

Directions: The graph below charts the sales of a book similar to *Girls Know Best*. Use the graph below to answer the questions.

Advertising the sale of a book can be difficult. The authors of the book, *Girls Know Best*, know just what this means. These young ladies have visited stores around the country and have autographed many books.

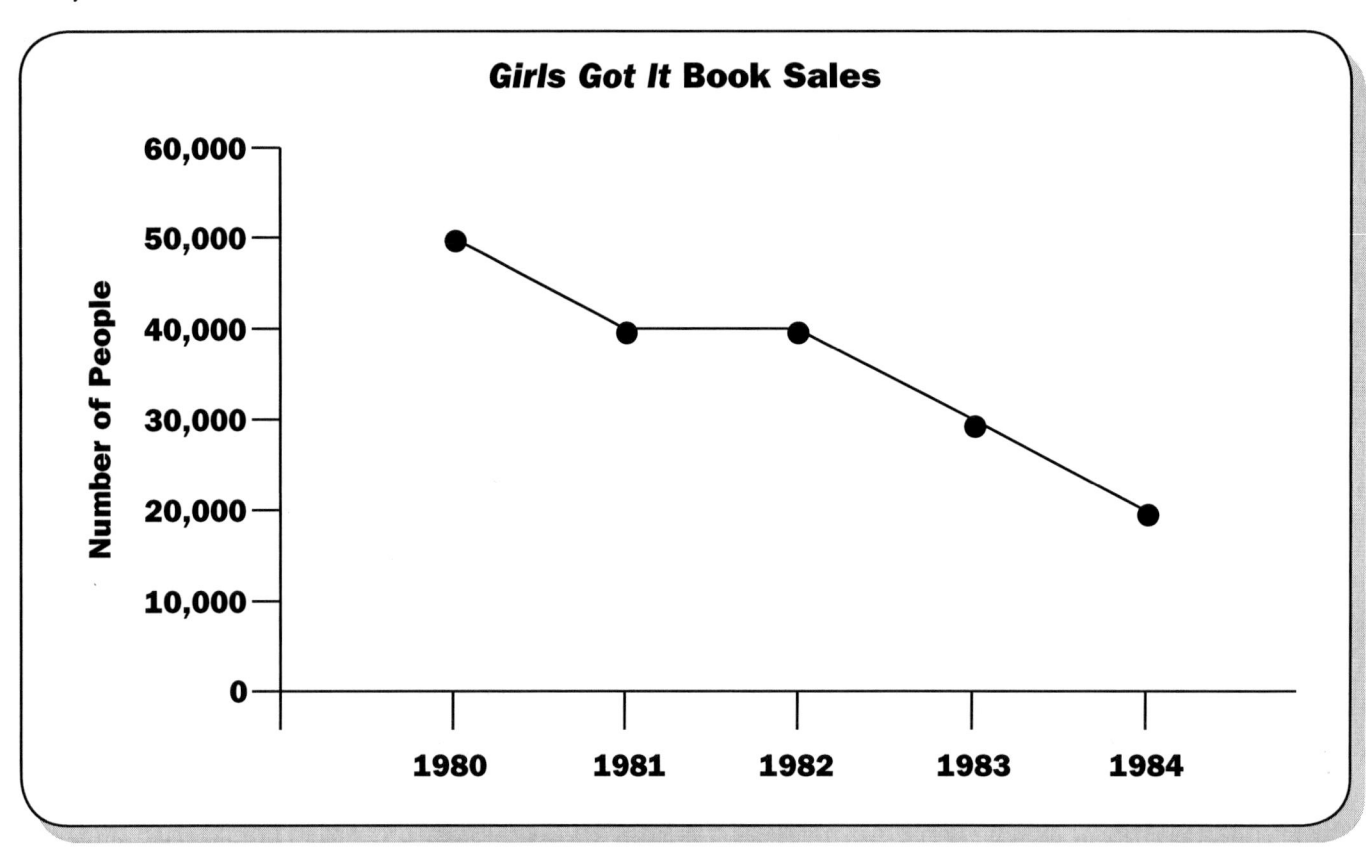

Girls Got It Book Sales

(Line graph — Number of People vs. Year)
- 1980: 50,000
- 1981: 40,000
- 1982: 40,000
- 1983: 30,000
- 1984: 20,000

1. What is the title of the book being advertised?

2. What number of people purchased the book in the year 1980?

3. What is the title of this graph?

4. What is the trend of sales looking like for this book in 1985?

5. How many more people bought the book in 1982 than in 1984?

Level 4

Lesson 5

Name_____ Date_____

Sentence Comprehension

Directions: Read the following sentence carefully and answer the questions below "True" (T) or "False" (F).

> Nobody likes a litterbug, but historians wish that Meriwether Lewis and William Clark had left more behind as they bravely traveled across the country over 200 years ago.

1. Lewis and Clark were litterbugs. _____
2. Historians wish they had more information about Lewis and Clark's expedition. _____
3. Lewis and Clark traveled across part of the United States. _____
4. Lewis and Clark were not brave enough on their expedition. _____
5. Lewis and Clark traveled over 200 years ago. _____

Word Study

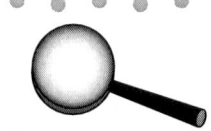

Directions: Correct the spelling of the underlined words in the sentences below.

> **ocian = ocean**
> William Clark spelled the word *ocean* as *ocian* in his diary. It has been mentioned that he was a horrible speller. There are many commonly misspelled words.

1. _____ The boys were getting into a lot of <u>mischeif</u>.

2. _____ There is a full moon <u>tomorow</u> night.

3. _____ The kids were so <u>embarased</u>.

4. _____ Mom was <u>makeing</u> fudge for our neighbors.

5. _____ Can you solve the <u>misteries</u> in the story?

6. _____ What are the <u>ansers</u> to the questions on the test?

©Shell Educational Publishing #10334 Nonfiction Comprehension Test Practice 45

Paragraph Comprehension

Directions: Read the paragraph below and answer the following questions.

> In 1803, President Thomas Jefferson asked Lewis to explore the Louisiana Purchase, a huge area of land that America was about to buy from France. He hoped to learn of a water route between the Mississippi River and the Pacific that would help the U.S. trade.

1. Who was asked to explore the Lousiana Purchase?
    a. William Clark
    b. Meriwether Lewis
    c. The country of France
    d. Thomas Jefferson

2. Who was president of the United States in 1803?
    a. Benjamin Franklin
    b. George Washington
    c. Thomas Jefferson
    d. John Quincy Adams

3. What was the intent of the trip?
    a. to determine the boundaries between the Mississippi River and the Pacific Ocean
    b. to determine the land and climate changes of the Louisiana Purchase
    c. to determine whether or not the United States should purchase Louisiana
    d. to learn of a water route between the Mississippi River and the Pacific Ocean

4. In what way would a water route aid the United States?
    a. trade
    b. exports
    c. imports
    d. future expeditions

5. The Americans were about to purchase the Lousiana Purchase from which country?
    a. France
    b. England
    c. Mexico
    d. Spain

Whole-Story Comprehension

Directions: Read the story below and answer the questions on the following page.

Hot on Lewis and Clark's Trail

Nobody likes a litterbug, but historians wish that Meriwether Lewis and William Clark had left more behind as they bravely traveled across the country over 200 years ago. They cleaned up so well that it's hard to tell exactly where they stopped on their historic journey from St. Louis, Missouri, to the Pacific Ocean.

Today, researchers are hot on the track of the explorers. They hope to answer age-old questions about these trailblazers of the West.

In 1803, President Thomas Jefferson asked Lewis to explore the Louisiana Purchase, a huge area of land that America was about to buy from France. He hoped to learn of a water route between the Mississippi River and the Pacific that would help the U.S. trade.

Lewis and his best friend, Clark, left St. Louis in May, 1804. They never found the water route, but they became the first U.S. citizens to see many of America's wonders—the endless Great Plains, the jagged Rocky Mountains, and the glittering Pacific. They faced many perils, including bear attacks and bitter cold. In Great Falls, Montana, they carried heavy canoes for weeks around waterfalls under the hot sun. At times, they were so hungry that they ate their pack horses.

More than 500 days and 4,000 miles after they had set out, Lewis and Clark reached the Pacific. "Ocian in view! O! the joy!" wrote Clark (a horrible speller) in his journal.

The explorers kept superb maps and diaries. They were the first to describe 122 kinds of animals, 178 plants, and many native tribes. But, they left barely a trace at their campsites. That makes it hard for historians to say, "Lewis and Clark were right here!"

Montana scientist Ken Karsmizki and others hope to pin down such facts. They are digging in the soil at Great Falls and Fort Clatsop, where the pair rested before making their separate ways home. Beads and gun ammunition were recently found at Fort Clatsop, but more tests are needed to prove they belonged to Lewis and Clark.

As the 200th anniversary of the journey arrived, Americans had plenty of chances to learn about the brave pioneers. PBS showed a film by Ken Burns and Dayton Duncan, who spent three years retracing the trip. A Lewis and Clark museum opened in Great Falls. Celebrations were held along the trail.

"When Lewis and Clark left, we were a seaboard collection of former colonies," says Burns. "What they saw transformed us from a small country into a great one."

Level 4   Lesson 5

Name_____ Date_____

Whole-Story Comprehension (cont.)

Directions: After you have read the story on the previous page, answer the questions below.

1. Who did Lewis invite on the trip?
   a. his brother, William Clark
   b. his mentor, Joseph Clark
   c. his father, William Clark
   d. his best friend, William Clark

2. What are some of the perils that Lewis and Clark faced?
   a. wild animals and wild birds
   b. bear attacks and bitter cold
   c. frigid waters and broken wagons
   d. lack of governmental support

3. Who was the poor speller?
   a. Meriwether Lewis
   b. Thomas Jefferson
   c. William Clark
   d. Joseph Clark

4. How long before Lewis and Clark reached the Pacific Ocean?
   a. 500 days and 4,000 miles
   b. 400 miles and 16 days
   c. 500 days and 5,000 miles
   d. 400 days and 5,000 miles

5. According to the article, what did Lewis and Clark discover and describe in their diaries?
   a. animals, plants, and native tribes
   b. animals and plants
   c. borders to Mexico and Canada
   d. native tribes and customs

6. Approximately how many years has it been since the expedition?
   a. over 300 years
   b. over 150 years
   c. 200 years
   d. 250 years

7. In connection with PBS, who has produced a film on the famous expedition?
   a. Ken Burns and Dayton Duncan
   b. Descendents of Lewis and Clark
   c. Ken Burns and William Clark
   d. Dayton Duncan and Meriwether Lewis

8. How are scientists able to learn more about Lewis and Clark's trip?
   a. They are interviewing family members.
   b. They are documenting evidence of the trip.
   c. They are digging in the soil where the pair rested before heading home.
   d. They are retracing the steps of Jefferson.

Enrichment

Directions: Read the following information and use it to add quotation marks to the sentences below.

> Dialogue and quotations are used to show when someone is speaking. Quotations are used in the article about Meriwether Lewis and William Clark. Using quotations can give more information on a topic and can give credence to facts and points the author is trying to make.
>
> - Knowing how to punctuate dialogue and quotations is important.
> - Place quotation marks directly before and after the quote.
> - Remember to write the name of the person who was quoted.
> - Periods and commas are always placed inside quotation marks.
> - Question marks and exclamation points are placed inside the quotation marks if it is part of the quote, but outside the quotation marks if it is part of the main sentence.

1. I thought they were an amazing pair, said Jane.

2. Lewis and Clark were anything but litterbugs, stated the teacher.

3. Where did Lewis and Clark start their journey? asked Fred.

4. Lewis and Clark began in Louisiana? questioned Sandy.

5. Mr. Roy asked, But where did they stop?

Name_____ Date_____

Graphic Development

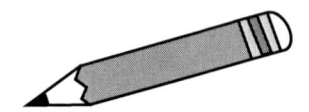

Directions: Use the map below to answer the following questions.

Lewis and Clark made their famous expedition in the year 1804. Neither of them knew the adventures they would face on the trip. As the 200th anniversary of the journey approached, people had a chance to learn more about this famous adventure.

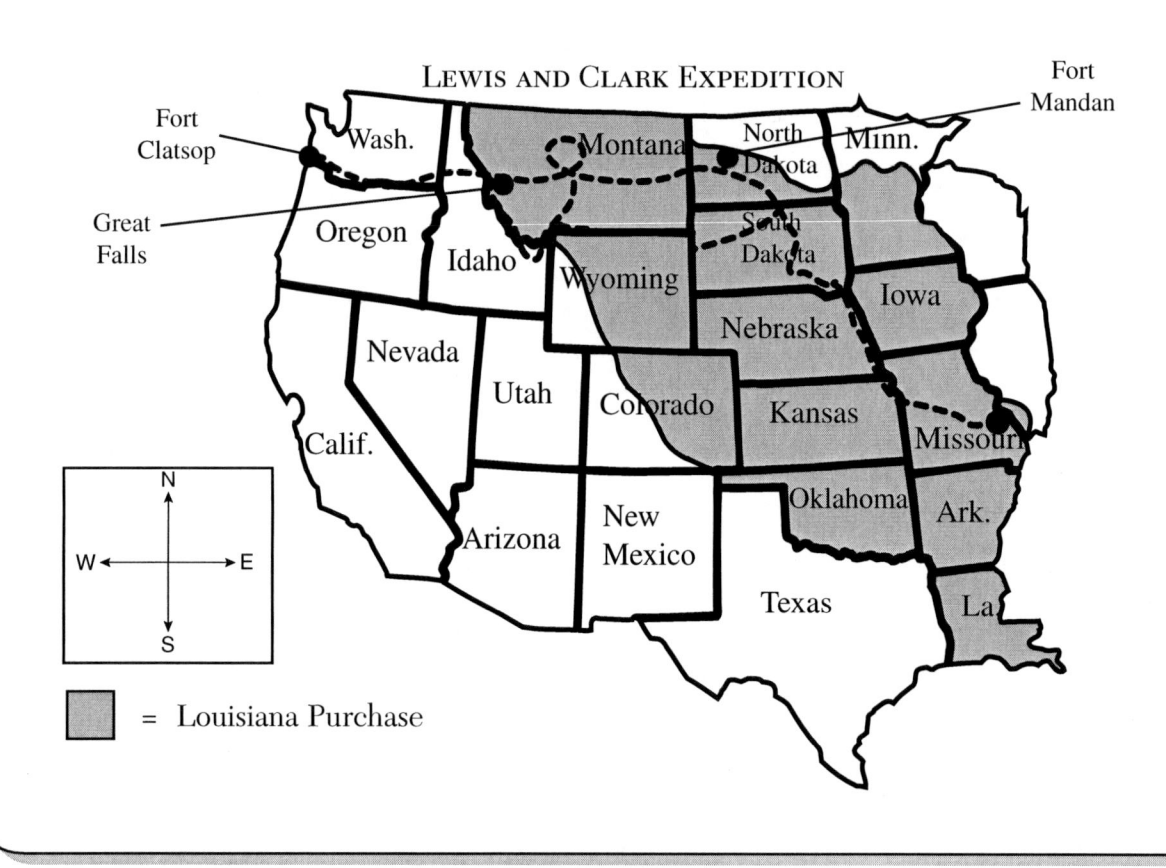

LEWIS AND CLARK EXPEDITION

(Map showing the Lewis and Clark Expedition route with Fort Clatsop, Great Falls, Fort Mandan labeled, and shaded states representing the Louisiana Purchase)

= Louisiana Purchase

1. What is the title of this map?
_____

2. Where did Lewis and Clark begin the expedition?
_____

3. In what direction did the pair head?
_____

4. How many states were part of the Louisiana Purchase?
_____

5. What are the names of the three places on the map that have dots next to them, indicating that Lewis and Clark stopped there temporarily?
_____

Level 4

Lesson 6

Name_____ Date_____

Sentence Comprehension

Directions: Read the following sentence carefully and answer the questions below "True" (T) or "False" (F).

> Both of the newly discovered creatures belong to a group of plant-eating dinosaurs called Ankylosaur, which means "fused lizards."

1. The newly discovered creatures are from the group Ankylosaur. _____
2. Both dinosaurs were meat-eaters. _____
3. The word Ankylosaur means "fused lizards." _____
4. The remains of the dinosaurs have recently been discovered. _____
5. The fused lizards were not considered dinosaurs. _____

Word Study

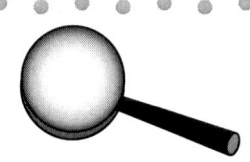

Directions: Look carefully at this table and then do the exercise.

> **million**
>
> A million is a very large number. *Millions* are usually associated with large masses of people, amounts of money, and distances.

A thousand has 3 zeros: 1,000
A million has 6 zeros: 1,000,000
A billion has 9 zeros: 1,000,000,000
A trillion has 12 zeros: 1,000,000,000,000

Now write the following numbers:

90 million: _____

64 million: _____

25 million: _____

90 billion: _____

2 trillion: _____

©Shell Educational Publishing   #10334 Nonfiction Comprehension Test Practice

Level 4   Lesson 6

Name_____ Date_____

Paragraph Comprehension

Directions: Read the paragraph below and answer the following questions.

> Most ankylosaurs lived 148 million to 64 million years ago, during the last dinosaur era, kown as the Late Cretaceous period. They lived in Asia and apparently crossed over to America on a land bridge that once connected Asia to what is now Alaska.

1. How many years ago did Ankylosaurs live?

  a. 148 million to 64 million years ago
  b. 142 million to 51 million years ago
  c. 153 million to 72 million years ago
  d. 164 million to 48 million years ago

2. The last dinosaur era is known as the

  a. Ceratopsian period.
  b. Early Jurassic period.
  c. Ornithischian period.
  d. Late Cretaceous period.

3. How do scientists think the Ankylosaurs got to America?

  a. They swam across the Atlantic Ocean.
  b. They crossed over through the mountains.
  c. They crossed over a land bridge.
  d. They were born in America.

4. From where did the Ankylosaurs originate?

  a. Alaska
  b. South America
  c. Asia
  d. Europe

5. The Ankylosaurs traveled to what is now

  a. Kansas.
  b. Alaska.
  c. Southern Arizona.
  d. The Everglades.

Whole-Story Comprehension

Directions: Read the story below and answer the questions on the following page.

A New Dino Duo

As a paleontologist, James Kirkland has examined thousands of different dinosaur bones. But even he wasn't prepared for what he saw when he was called to investigate some new fossils found near Salt Lake City, Utah. A fossil bed there held the bones of two never-before-seen species of Ankylosaur. The discovery is changing scientists' ideas about the history of dinosaurs in America.

Both of the newly discovered creatures belong to a group of plant-eating dinosaurs called Ankylosaur, which means "fused lizards." The name comes from the heavy armor-like plates attached or fused to their heads. Some grew more than 30 feet long.

"These two dinosaurs were very similar animals in many respects," says Kirkland. One is an Ankylosaurid. An Ankylosaurid had big armored plates around the head and a long tail with a heavy club at the end. It would swing the club tail to fight bigger animals, like the Tyrannosaurus Rex.

The other new species, the Nodosaurid, was also well armed. "It had spikes on its shoulders that it used to ram larger creatures," says Kirkland. "These dinosaurs were built like tanks."

Most Ankylosaurs lived 148 million to 64 million years ago, during the last dinosaur era, known as the Late Cretaceous period. They lived in Asia and apparently crossed over to America on a land bridge that once connected Asia to what is now Alaska.

"Ankylosauria was in a real hurry to get over here from Asia," says Kirkland. "They were some of the first to get here."

By studying volcanic ash found near the site, scientists have determined that the Ankylosaurid bones were 25 million years older than any other known American Ankylosaur. This means that the land bridge must have existed earlier than scientists had believed. Paleontologist Kenneth Carpenter says these findings push the date that the land bridge existed back from 90 million years ago to 110 million years ago.

The skull and armor of the Ankylosaurid and the shoulder blade of the Nodosaurid are being studied by experts at the College of Eastern Utah Prehistoric Museum. Already they have learned that the head armor of the Ankylosaurid is not a bunch of plates attached to its head, but an outgrowth of its skull bones. They are eager to discover more about these armed warriors of a lost world.

Level 4   Lesson 6

Name_____ Date_____

Whole-Story Comprehension (cont.)

Directions: After you have read the story on the previous page, answer the questions below.

1. Who is James Kirkland?
   a. a scientist who studies lizards
   b. a professor
   c. a paleontologist
   d. a doctor

2. The discovery of these fossils is changing scientists' ideas about what?
   a. the history of the land bridge
   b. the history of the earth
   c. the beginning of fossil fuels
   d. the history of dinosaurs

3. The word Ankylosaur means
   a. fused lizards.
   b. lizards with caps.
   c. lizards with extra legs.
   d. lizards with shells.

4. From what does the name "fused lizards" come?
   a. the spikes on the head
   b. the heavy armor-like plates
   c. the fusing of two lizards
   d. the legs of the lizard, fused together

5. The Ankylosaurids would fight bigger animals such as
   a. a Stegosaurus.
   b. a Bronchosaurus.
   c. a Tyrannosaurus Rex.
   d. an Achranid.

6. What did the scientists study to determine that the bones were 25 million years old?
   a. the armor-like plates
   b. the land bridge
   c. the dinosaur fossils
   d. volcanic ash

7. The land bridge must have existed_____ than scientists believed.
   a. later
   b. earlier
   c. in a larger scale
   d. closer to Asia

8. What have scientists learned about the head armor?
   a. They learned it broke off easily.
   b. They learned it was also found on the Tyrannosaurus Rex.
   c. They learned that the armor is not a bunch of plates attached to its head, but an outgrowth of skull bones.
   d. They learned it was cartilage instead of bones.

54   #10334 Nonfiction Comprehension Test Practice   ©Shell Educational Publishing

Enrichment

Directions: Read the following information and use it to match the words with the definitions below.

James Kirkland is a scientist who studies dinosaur bones. He is called a *paleontologist*. A paleontologist studies a science called *paleontology*. There are many words that end in "ology." The suffix "ology" means "the science of" or "the study of" something. For example, *mineralogy* is the study of *minerals*. Many of these words are used when studying social studies and science.

Words   **Definitions**

1. _____ meteorology   A. Study of insects

2. _____ biology   B. Study of fruit

3. _____ cytology   C. Study of poisons

4. _____ dermatology   D. Study of ancestors

5. _____ pomology   E. Study of cells

6. _____ genealogy   F. Study of life

7. _____ entomology   G. Study of weather

8. _____ sociology   H. Study of skin

9. _____ toxicology   I. Study of society

Level 4 | Lesson 6

Name_____ Date_____

Graphic Development

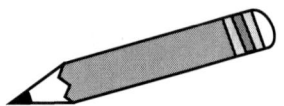

Directions: Dinosaurs lived millions of years ago. There are many different eras that date back millions of years. The dinosaurs were part of the Mesozoic Era. Use the chart below to answer the questions.

Dating Dinosaurs
(mya = million years ago)

Phanerozoic Eon (544 mya to present)	Cenozoic Era (65 mya to today)	Quaternary (1.8 mya to today)
		    Holocene (11,000 mya to today)
		    Plestocene (1.8 mya to 11,000 yrs.)
		Tertiary (65 to 1.8 mya)
		    Pliocene (5 to 1.8 mya)
		    Miocene (23 to 5 mya)
		    Oligocene (38 to 23 mya)
		    Eocene (54 to 38 mya)
		    Paleocene (65 to 54 mya)

	Mesozoic Era (245 to 65 mya)	Cretaceous (146 to 65 mya) Jurassic (208 to 146 mya) Triassic (245 to 208 mya)

	Paleozoic Era (544 to 245 mya)	Permian (286 to 245 mya)
		Carboniferous (360 to 286 mya)
		    Pennsylvanian (325 to 286 mya)
		    Mississippian (360 to 325 mya)
		Devonian (410 to 360 mya)
		Silurian (440 to 410 mya)
		Ordovician (505 to 440 mya)
		Cambrian (544 to 505 mya)
		Tommotian (530 to 528 mya)

Precambrian Time (4,500 to 544 mya)	Proterozoic Era (2,500 to 544 mya)	Neoproterozoic (900 to 544 mya) Vendian (650 to 544 mya) Mesoproterozoic (1,600 to 900 mya) Paleoproterozoic (2,500 to 1,600 mya)
	Archaean (3,800 to 2,500 mya)	
	Hadean (450 to 3,800 mya)	

1. What is the title of the chart? _____

2. What do the letters mya stand for? _____

3. In what era were Cretaceous, Jurassic, and Triassic periods? _____

4. How many million years ago was the Proterozoic Era? _____

5. What era was 65 million years ago until today? _____

56   #10334 Nonfiction Comprehension Test Practice   ©Shell Educational Publishing

Level 4　　　　　　　　　　　　　　　　　　　　　　　　　　　　　　　　　Lesson 7

Name_____　Date_____

Sentence Comprehension

Directions: Read the following sentence carefully and answer the questions below "True" (T) or "False" (F).

> In a chairlift ride, kids can pull their family and friends 30 feet up in the air, then let them free-fall back down.

1. The ride takes people up 40 feet in the air. _____
2. The people in the chairlift ride free-fall down. _____
3. Adults must operate the machines. _____
4. Shooting the family into space for 2 hours is a feature of the chairlift ride. _____
5. The chairlift ride is operated by the kids. _____

Word Study

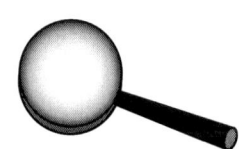

Directions: Some words can be joined to form compound words. Put the words below together and write a brief meaning of the compound word.

toymaker

A toymaker designs and creates toys. Toymaker is also a *compound word*. A *compound word* is two separate words combined together to form a new word. The meaning of the new word usually has something to do with the separate words, but a *compound word* does take on a meaning of its own.

1. news + paper　　compound word = _____

   meaning = _____

2. cow + boy　　　compound word = _____

   meaning = _____

3. hair + net　　　compound word = _____

   meaning = _____

4. home + bound　compound word = _____

   meaning = _____

©Shell Educational Publishing　　　　　　　　　#10334 Nonfiction Comprehension Test Practice

Level 4 Lesson 7

Name_____ Date_____

Paragraph Comprehension

Directions: Read the paragraph below and answer the following questions.

> Watching LEGOs being made is just one of the attractions at Legoland California, a new theme park in Carlsbad, California. Legoland has rides and shows, but what makes it special is its amazing Lego constructions.

1. Where is LEGOLAND located in California?
   a. San Diego
   b. Los Angeles
   c. Newport Beach
   d. Carlsbad

2. What makes LEGOLAND special?
   a. The fact that it is a theme park.
   b. The fact that it is now open to the public.
   c. There are amazing LEGO constructions.
   d. The fact that kids are welcome at this theme park.

3. What could you expect to do at LEGOLAND?
   a. You can expect to see the largest whales there.
   b. You can expect to meet the president of the LEGO company.
   c. You can expect to meet famous characters there.
   d. You can expect to go on rides, see shows, and see amazing LEGO constructions.

4. What do you think a theme park is?
   a. a place where kids are welcome
   b. a park with activities and shows connected to a theme
   c. a park that is built in a large city, usually in California
   d. a park that has themes and toys to play with

5. What is made at LEGOLAND?
   a. LEGOs
   b. legs
   c. action figures
   d. LEGO containers

Lesson 7

ARTICLE FROM TIME FOR KIDS

Name_____ Date_____

Whole Story-Comprehension

Directions: Read the story below and answer the questions on the following page.

LEGOLAND

The machine cranks up and 450 degrees of fiery heat turns bright plastic to mush. Then the machine applies 150 tons of pressure to the plastic. Ten seconds later, out comes a LEGO, one of those molded-plastic building blocks you can combine to build almost anything, from a spaceship to a dragon.

Watching LEGOs being made is just one of the attractions at LEGOLAND California, a new theme park in Carlsbad, California. LEGOLAND has rides and shows, but what makes it special is its amazing LEGO constructions.

Master LEGO builders used two million blocks to create a 34-foot-long red dinosaur that towers above LEGOLAND Lake. More than one million blocks form the giant face of Albert Einstein in the park's Imagination Zone. More than 20 million were used to create incredibly detailed mini-versions of such great American cities as New Orleans, Washington, D.C., and New York City!

The California park is the first LEGOLAND park in the U.S. The original LEGOLAND opened in 1968 in Denmark. Danish toymaker Ole Kirk Christiansen invented the bright bricks more than 50 years ago. Since then, more than 189 billion have been made. That's almost 30 LEGO pieces for every person on the planet.

Nearly all of the 40 attractions at LEGOLAND California look like giant LEGOS. The rides don't move unless the kids make them work. Where else can you drive a LEGO boat or an electric LEGO car and get your own LEGO license? In a chairlift ride, kids can pull their family and friends 30 feet up in the air, then let them free-fall back down.

"Most parks are for everybody," says LEGOLAND spokeswoman Jonna Rae Barteges. "This whole park is just for kids."

Whole-Story Comprehension (cont.)

Directions: After you have read the story on the previous page, answer the questions below.

1. What type of machine is being described in the first paragraph?
   a. one of the rides at LEGOLAND
   b. a giant face of Albert Einstein
   c. one of the constructions at LEGOLAND
   d. a LEGO-making machine

2. What types of things would you find on a brochure advertising LEGOLAND?
   a. the rides, shows, and LEGOLAND constructions
   b. the boat rides, the dinosaurs, and the kid-operated machines
   c. the newly built theme park in Denmark
   d. the inventor of LEGOs

3. Which cities have mini-versions made of them using LEGOs at LEGOLAND?
   a. New York City and Washington, D.C.
   b. New Orleans, New York City, and Washington, D.C.
   c. New Hampshire, New York, and New Orleans
   d. Chicago, New Orleans, and New York City

4. Who created the 34-foot-long dinosaur?
   a. scientists that make LEGOs
   b. children from nearby cities
   c. master LEGO builders
   d. kids that won a contest

5. Where and when was the first LEGOLAND built?
   a. Los Angeles, CA, in 1978
   b. Phoenix, AZ, in 1968
   c. Sweden in 2000
   d. Denmark in 1968

6. How many pieces of LEGOs have been made?
   a. 189 billion
   b. 150 billion
   c. 400 billion
   d. too many to count

7. For whom is LEGOLAND targeted?
   a. girls between 5–10
   b. boys between 5–10
   c. kids
   d. none of the above

8. How many years ago were LEGOs invented?
   a. a century ago
   b. over a half of a century ago
   c. a quarter of a century ago
   d. none of the above

Enrichment

Directions: Read the information below and use it to answer the following questions.

Where in the World is LEGOLAND?

Years ago, when people heard the term LEGOLAND, they would have wondered where it was and who lived in that land. Now all kids know that LEGOLAND is a place of fun and adventure, filled with LEGOs. As new products and new items are invented, new terms and new uses of old words have been adopted into the English language.

Look at these examples of "new" words, just as a result of technology:

Browser: This is a tool or program that allows you to search the Web. The most common Web browsers used today are *Netscape Navigator* and *Internet Explorer.*

Chat Room: People from all over can "chat" with others online on a variety of subjects. You need to be careful about using chat rooms. Dangerous people sometimes get involved with chat rooms.

Cyberspace: This is another word for the Internet.

Download: This is transferring information or files from the Internet to your computer. You must be careful when downloading. This is how computer viruses are spread.

FAQ: This is the abbreviation for "frequently asked questions." There is usually a category under the help section for these questions on Web sites.

Online: This is when you are using the Internet. You are then online.

Search Engine: Search engines are helpful when researching topics.

Surfing: This is what you are doing when you are looking around on the Internet.

URL: A URL is the address of a Web site. You must be very specific and type the exact letters of an address. You cannot add spaces or letters that don't appear in the address.

Write the word from each sentence that is the "new" word or new use of an old word.

1. _____ The CD has a scratch in it.
2. _____ How many megabytes does your computer have?
3. _____ What is the URL for that Web site?
4. _____ They built a tower using LEGOs.
5. _____ The movie was a DVD, not a video.

Graphic Development

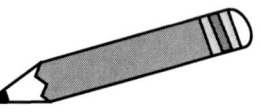

Directions: The new LEGOLAND theme park is now open and running. It is located in Carlsbad, California. But just where is Carlsbad? Look closely at the map and answer the questions below.

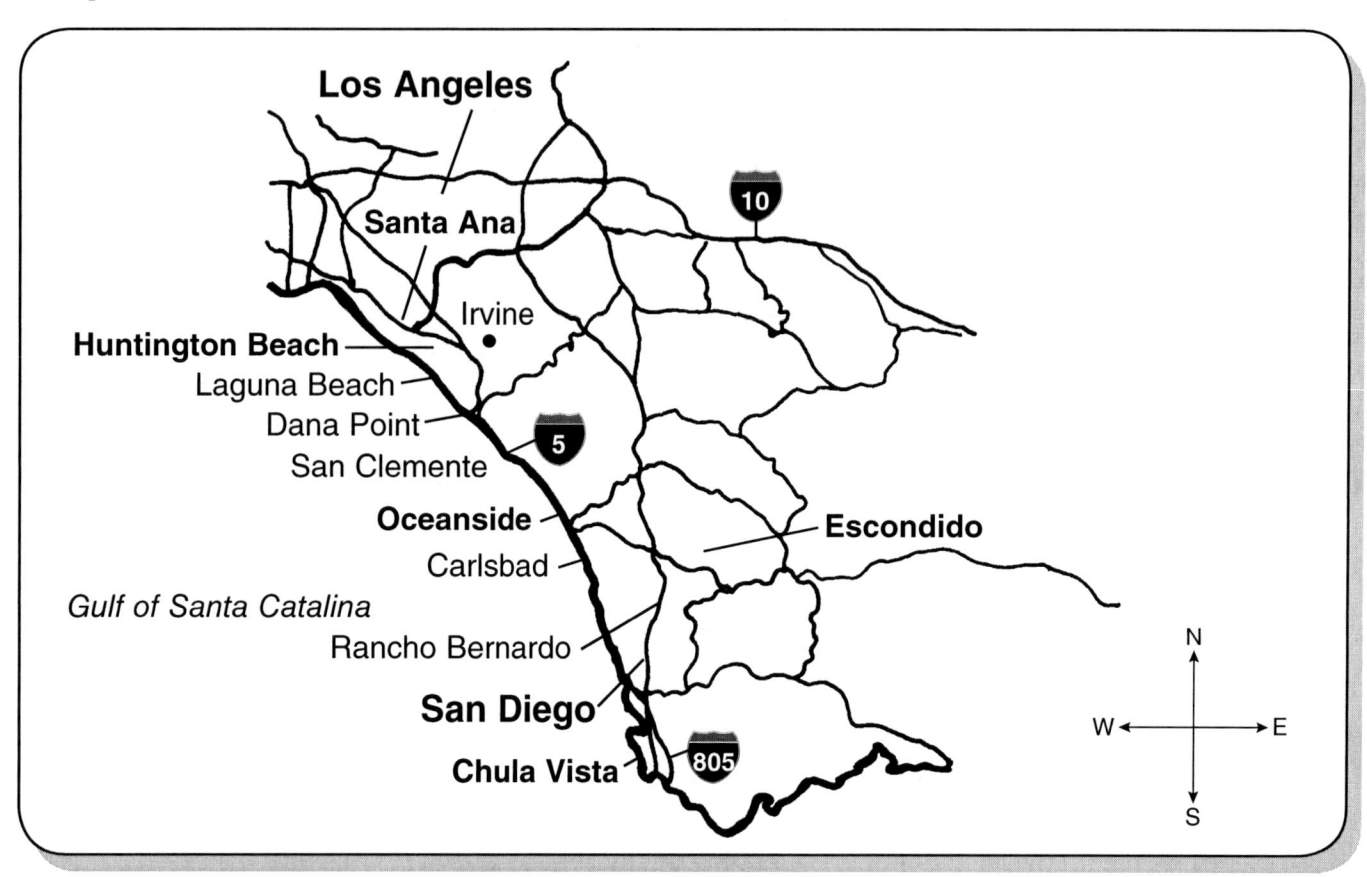

1. What gulf is Carlsbad, CA, next to?

2. Is LEGOLAND north or south of Sea World in San Diego, CA?

3. Is Carlsbad, CA, one of California's larger or smaller cities?

4. If a person lived in Los Angeles, which direction would he or she be heading to get to LEGOLAND?

5. What interstate runs through Carlsbad, CA?

Sentence Comprehension

Directions: Read the following sentence carefully and answer the questions below "True" (T) or "False" (F).

> Writer Laurie Stroblas began the District Lines Poetry Project in 1994, hoping to give bus riders something better to stare at than ads or graffiti.

1. Laurie Stroblas is a student in Washington, D.C. _____
2. The poetry would replace ads and graffiti. _____
3. The District Lines Poetry Project began in 1994. _____
4. The project was to give bus riders something inspiring to read. _____
5. The project was intended to curb violence in the subways. _____

Word Study

Directions: Match the correct definition with the italicized homograph in each sentence.

board

Board is a word that has two definitions. *Board* can mean a piece of sawed lumber, but in this article it means to get on board or enter, as in boarding the subway. These two words are called *homographs*. Homographs are words that are spelled the same but have different meanings and origins.

a. boil—bubbling of hot liquid
b. boil—red swelling on the skin
c. bark—tree covering
d. bark—sound a dog makes
e. arms—body parts
f. arms—weapons
g. bank—land along a river
h. bank—place of financial business

_____ 1. The *bank* was slippery and covered with moss.
_____ 2. His *bark* grew louder and louder as the darkness came.
_____ 3. The *boil* on her arm was painful and sore.
_____ 4. Greg is planning to use his *arms* to support the weight of the box.
_____ 5. Please take this check and deposit it at the *bank*.
_____ 6. You can stop stirring once it begins to *boil*.

Level 4　　　　　　　　　　　　　　　　　　　　　　　　　　　　　　Lesson 8

Name_____ Date_____

Paragraph Comprehension

Directions: Read the paragraph below and answer the following questions.

> "The response was incredible," says Stroblas. Last year, she decided to transfer her idea to the buses and picked new poems with the advice of 150 students. Organizations donated enough money to keep Metro Muse in subway stations all winter. In spring, a new crop of poems sprouted on city buses.

1. How did Stroblas get the money she needed to post the poems?

　　a. She held fund raisers to earn the money.
　　b. She gathered donations from willing parents.
　　c. Organizations donated the money.
　　d. The local PTA donated and raised money for the project.

2. What number of students helped pick new poems?

　　a. 1,500 students
　　b. 150 students
　　c. all the middle school students
　　d. 12 students

3. What was the response to the project like?

　　a. not enough interest and so it was canceled
　　b. mediocre, not much interest
　　c. incredible
　　d. none of the above

4. How were the poems selected?

　　a. with the advice of students
　　b. by a drawing
　　c. The community voted.
　　d. none of the above

5. When did a new crop of poems show up on city buses?

　　a. next year
　　b. in the spring
　　c. next month
　　d. when enough money had been raised to fund the project

Lesson 8

Name_____ Date_____

Whole-Story Comprehension

Directions: Read the story below and answer the questions on the following page.

The Poetry Express

Jazzy new signs in subway stations have been catching the eyes of commuters in Washington, D.C. Instead of rushing to board a train, people pause to read poems written by kids.

The lighted posters, called "Metro Muse," appeared at 10 train stops in the busy city. On display: 12 thoughtful compositions to celebrate kids' creativity and to promote reading.

Writer Laurie Stroblas began the District Lines Poetry Project in 1994, hoping to give bus riders something better to stare at than ads or graffiti. She had been leading poetry workshops in public schools, so she asked her students to lend a hand.

"The response was incredible," says Stroblas. Later, she decided to transfer her ideas to the buses and picked new poems with the advice of 150 students. Organizations donated enough money to keep Metro Muse in subway stations all winter. In spring, a new crop of poems sprouted on city buses.

What were the poems about? Snow falling, the arrival of a new year, love, fear, and peace. Cindy Rosales, a sixth grader at Oyster Elementary School, was inspired by her favorite type of music: "Kindness is the jazz," she wrote. "Bring the big jazz in. The big, whole jazz."

Like most poets, the kids had mixed feelings about letting the public read their private thoughts. "I would feel glad that someone read my poem," one girl said. "But I would feel sad if they missed their train."

Level 4   Lesson 8

Name_____   Date_____

Whole-Story Comprehension *(cont.)*

Directions: After you have read the story on the previous page, answer the questions below.

1. Where are the poems posted?
    a. subway stations and trains
    b. subway stations and buses
    c. on the school grounds
    d. in the classroom

2. What is the occupation of Laurie Stroblas?
    a. a doctor
    b. a teacher
    c. a politician
    d. a writer and a teacher

3. What are some of the topics of the poems?
    a. death, hatred, and war
    b. love, fear, and peace
    c. school, tests, and fighting
    d. hope, fear, and rain

4. The District Lines Poetry Project was
    a. started in 1995.
    b. initiated by Laurie Stroblas.
    c. ordered to begin by the President.
    d. first for the parents and now for the kids.

5. What is the purpose of the Poetry Project?
    a. It promotes reading and spotlights children's creativity.
    b. It keeps children out of gangs.
    c. It supports the school's after school programs.
    d. It is the first of its kind to include the writings of teachers.

6. Select a new title that best fits the information in this article.
    a. The Poetry Pizza
    b. Kids First – Poetry Second
    c. Here Comes the Bus!
    d. The Metro Muse

7. Students have received inspiration for the poetry from
    a. ideas brainstormed as a class.
    b. other poems posted in the subway.
    c. music, personal thoughts, and experiences.
    d. poetry books.

8. How do the students feel about letting others read their poems?
    a. There are mixed feelings.
    b. All the kids are excited.
    c. The kids don't want the public to read their poems.
    d. none of the above

Level 4   Lesson 8

Name_____ Date_____

Enrichment

Directions: Read the information below and use it to answer the following questions.

Poetry is music to the ears. Poetry also provides a means to express thoughts, feelings, and ideas. The Metro Muse posters at 10 train stops in Washington are proof of the inspiration and positive feelings that poetry offers.

Language has rhythm and poetry taps into that rhythm. Consider the poem by sixth-grader Cindy Rosales, from "The Poetry Express":

> "Kindess is the jazz.
>
> Bring the big jazz in.
>
> The big,
>
> Whole jazz."

The words do not rhyme, as is often thought of with poetry, and yet, the words come to life and bring a rhyme of their own. Another type of rhythm with words is *alliteration*. Alliteration is the repetition of the beginning sound of two or more words in a sentence. Alliteration is often used with descriptions. Read the following examples of alliteration:

- A sleek, shiny red car slid into the driveway.
- A bold and brassy young lady bounced into the room.
- The cute, cuddly kitten came to where I sat.
- A bright and beautiful sun was beaming down this morning.

Circle the number beside each sentence that uses alliteration.

1. A brilliantly-beautiful baby bird sat up on the branch.

2. A red and green sailboat came into view.

3. The peaceful poem inspired hope and promise.

4. The song was a loud and noisy one.

5. A busy bumble bee buzzed boldly toward us.

Level 4   **Lesson 8**

Name_____ Date_____

Graphic Development

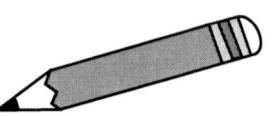

Directions: The poetry of children adorns the walls of subways and train stops in Washington to give riders something different to look at other than advertisements or graffiti. In metropolitan areas, signs are plentiful. Signs use symbols to carry the message to others. Interpret the symbols on the signs below.

1.

_____

2.

_____

3.

_____

4.

_____

5.

_____

Lesson 9

Level 4

Name_____ Date_____

Sentence Comprehension

Directions: Read the following sentence carefully and answer the questions below "True" (T) or "False" (F).

> In 1998, 181 million video and computer games were sold in the U.S.

1. In 1998, there were many computer and video games sold. _____
2. Only video games are allowed to be sold in the U.S. _____
3. Computer games are considered illegal. _____
4. Video games and computer games could be considered popular. _____
5. Not very many video and computer games were sold in 1998. _____

Word Study

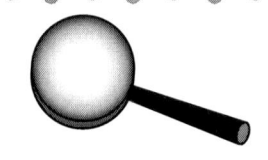

Directions: Locate all the proper nouns in the paragraph below and write them on the lines using capital letters.

Missouri

Missouri is one of fifty states in the United States of America. Missouri is a proper noun. A proper noun is different than a common noun. A proper noun is the name of a specific person, place, or thing. Proper nouns are always capitalized.

sandy was able to come visit us in november. It was cool outside and we were excited to jump in the leaves again. She always comes to visit us and grandma nan this time of year. It just wouldn't seem like thanksgiving without her. We really enjoy having her and her dog heidi come to see us.

1. _____
2. _____
3. _____
4. _____
5. _____
6. _____

©Shell Educational Publishing

Paragraph Comprehension

Directions: Read the paragraph below and answer the following questions.

> Surprisingly, experts who study kids and video games say games are not all bad. Some games build problem-solving skills. Unfortunately, kids can go overboard.

1. Unfortunately, what do kids do with video games?
   a. They can't figure out how to play the video games.
   b. They play them so much, the video games break.
   c. They go overboard and play them too much.
   d. They don't have enough time to play the video games.

2. Experts say that
   a. every family should have at least one video game.
   b. not all video games are bad.
   c. children aren't old enough to be playing video games.
   d. parents should be playing the video games with their children.

3. Video and computer games can be positive when
   a. they build problem-solving skills.
   b. they contain the basic nutrients and vitamins.
   c. they build self-esteem.
   d. they teach kids how to play fairly.

4. Experts have studied kids
   a. in Europe.
   b. and their parents.
   c. and computers.
   d. and video games.

5. Going overboard means
   a. jumping off the couch in the middle of a video game.
   b. eating all of your meals and playing video games at the same time.
   c. doing your homework before you play a video game.
   d. spending too much time watching and playing video games.

Whole-Story Comprehension

Directions: Read the story below and answer the questions on the following page.

Hooked!

It's 10 A.M. on a Saturday. Ricky Picone, 11, and his brother David, 10, are soaked in sweat. Two seconds remain in the game, and David is up by one point. Ricky grabs the ball. He shoots; he scores! "Game over. You lose!" shouts Ricky.

A morning basketball game? Sort of. Except Ricky and David are in their basement and still in pajamas. They are playing video basketball. Their parents have been calling them to come up for breakfast for 25 minutes. Mom and Dad are not too happy.

Sound familiar? No wonder. Video games are big in kids' lives, and in some cases they've taken over!

In 2004, 248 million video and computer games costing 7.3 billion dollars were sold in the U.S. That's over two games for every household. With all the cool new games, some kids can't stop playing.

You know the kids. They are the ones who spend more time with video games than eating or sleeping. "There's this one kid," says John Szendiuch, 12, of Pelham, New York, "they're his whole life."

When kids play all the time, parents become upset. Ron Hughes of Missouri found that he couldn't even talk to his son Russell, 9, when he was playing a video game. "The phone would ring," says Hughes, "and Russell wouldn't hear it."

Parents also worry about violence. The blood-gushing in many video games is enough to make some parents ban all video games. Surprisingly, experts who study kids and video games say games are not all bad. Some games build problem-solving skills. Unfortunately, kids can go overboard.

How do kids and parents keep playing under control? "It's important for parents to take an interest in what kids are playing," says expert David Walsh. "Then parents can make fair rules and understand why kids love the games."

Walsh believes parents must limit kids' playing time. He recommends no more than 90 minutes a day. But watch out! Kids are going to want to play even more. Video games are becoming bigger, brighter, and even harder for kids to resist.

Whole-Story Comprehension (cont.)

Directions: After you have read the story on the previous page, answer the questions below.

1. The parents in this article feel
   a. happy and excited.
   b. excited and frustrated.
   c. confused and angry.
   d. frustrated and unhappy.

2. What has taken over the lives of some kids?
   a. the video games they play
   b. the television set
   c. the amount of homework they are required to do
   d. none of the above

3. Parents are concerned about the _____ in some video games.
   a. nudity
   b. violence
   c. language
   d. songs

4. What is the occupation of David Walsh?
   a. He makes video games.
   b. He is a scientific expert.
   c. He is a teacher.
   d. He is a concerned parent.

5. What does David Walsh recommend to parents?
   a. destroying all video games
   b. teaching children how to budget the money they spend on video games
   c. to take an interest in what kids are playing and setting limits
   d. buying more video games so that each child has a turn to play

6. Why do you think kids have a hard time playing the video games for short periods of time?
   a. The kids don't like to watch TV.
   b. The kids get hooked into a game and can't stop.
   c. The kids want to disobey their parents.
   d. The kids are trying to set the record for the amount of time they play the video games.

7. What do you think are some of the down sides of becoming so involved in playing the video and computer games?
   a. It's hard to take turns.
   b. There isn't enough time to play all the video games the kids have.
   c. The kids spend all of their time playing video games instead of talking with family and having a normal life.
   d. none of the above

8. What is the recommended number of minutes suggested by experts?
   a. 100 minutes
   b. no more than 90 minutes
   c. no more than 50 minutes
   d. no more than 20 minutes

Enrichment

Directions: Read the information below and use it to answer the following questions.

It is obvious from the article on kids playing video and computer games that there is concern about the effects and the time spent playing these games. Parents often have a difficult time setting limits and getting the correct message sent to their kids. Sometimes parents say one thing, but kids interpret it to mean a different thing. This is where many of the parent/child conflicts happen. It's all in the interpretation of what we are saying.

In writing, there are two different kinds of meanings of the words you use. The **denotation** of a word is the meaning that you would find in the dictionary. The **connotation** of a word is the feeling or mental picture that people associate with the word.

For example, the words *notorious* and *famous* have different connotations. Notorious has a negative connotation. It makes you think that a person is well-known for bad or outrageous things. Famous suggests that a person is well known for all the good and wonderful things he or she did.

Here are some examples of connotations used in the article, "Hooked!" that you just read. The italicized words are taken from the article.

Negative words	**Positive Words**
grabs	takes
addicted	*hooked*
violence	aggression
mad	upset

Label each of the words below. Write positive or negative to describe its connotation.

1. _____ instantly/hastily _____

2. _____ debate/quarrel _____

3. _____ odor/fragrance _____

4. _____ snoop/investigate _____

5. _____ attract/lure _____

6. _____ call/yell _____

Graphic Development

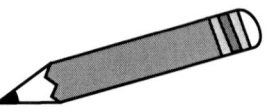

Directions: Read the following information and then use the double line graph below to answer the questions.

More and more young people are playing video and computer games. Some say the habit is addictive. In 2004, 248 million video and computer games were sold in the United States.

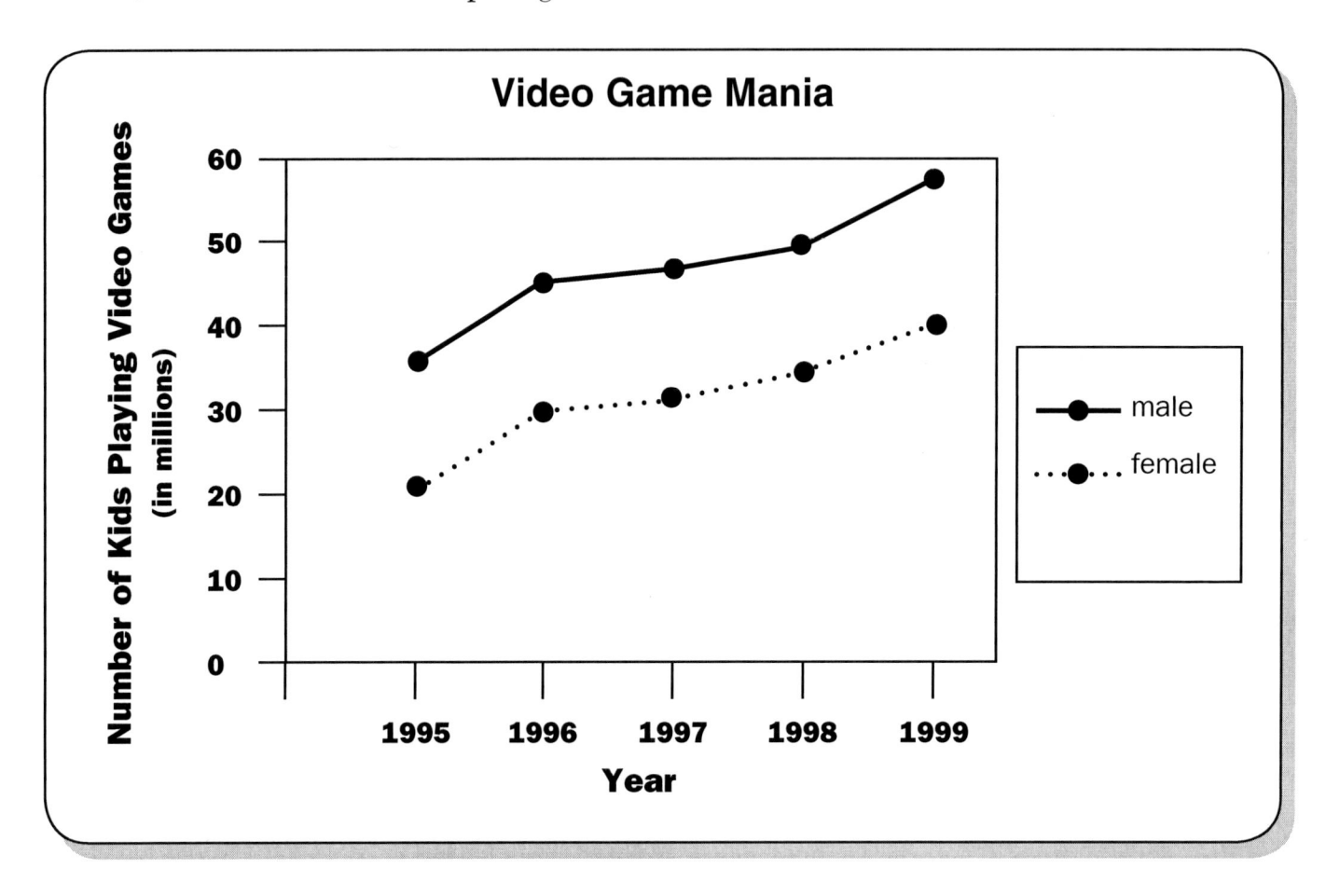

Video Game Mania

Number of Kids Playing Video Games (in millions) vs. Year (1995-1999); male and female

1. What does this graph show?
   _____

2. What number of males played video games in 1997?
   _____

3. What is the title of this graph?
   _____

4. How many more males than females played video games in 1995?
   _____

5. How many more males played video games in 1999 compared to 1995?
   _____

Level 4
Lesson 10

Name_____ Date_____

Sentence Comprehension

Directions: Read the following sentence carefully and answer the questions below "True" (T) or "False" (F).

> People who are allergic to peanuts must avoid anything containing a peanut or its oil.

1. People can be allergic to peanuts. _____
2. People must avoid anything containing almond oil. _____
3. If people are allergic to peanuts, they should also avoid peanut oil. _____
4. All people are allergic to peanut oil. _____
5. An allergy to peanuts means you can't eat things with peanuts. _____

Word Study

Directions: Find six words below that have three syllables like the word sacrifice. Write these three-syllable words on the lines that follow.

sacrifice
Sacrifice means to give up something for the sake of something else. Sacrifice is a word that has three syllables. A syllable is a unit of spoken language. In the dictionary, syllables are denoted with a dot or a hyphen between each syllable. Syllables aid in the pronunciation of a word.

amazing	curious	seaport	agriculture	nutritious
doubtful	science	together	interesting	misspelled
projects	height	mothering	bring	sandwiches

1. _____
2. _____
3. _____
4. _____
5. _____
6. _____

Name_____   Date_____

Paragraph Comprehension

Directions: Read the paragraph below and answer the following questions.

> Banning peanut butter creates some sticky problems. Peanut-butter-and-jelly sandwiches are popular. They are nutritious, affordable food for most families. However, there are many choices for a healthful lunch. School cafeterias can provide a wide choice of foods that are safe for all kids. They can even send home suggestions for bag lunches that don't include peanuts. People should be willing to sacrifice a particular food if it might save a child's life. All schools should ban peanuts and peanut products.

1. Which type of sandwich is considered popular, but deadly to some kids?

    a. ham sandwiches

    b. sardine sandwiches

    c. jelly and cheese sandwiches

    d. peanut-butter-and-jelly sandwiches

2. Who could provide healthy and safe alternatives?

    a. the cafeterias

    b. the teachers

    c. the students that are allergic to peanuts

    d. the parents of the students

3. The author is ultimately trying to persuade schools to what?

    a. keep kids from getting allergies

    b. ban peanuts and peanut products from school

    c. build more playground equipment for students with allergies

    d. address the needs of all students with allergies

4. According to the article, who should ban peanuts and peanut products?

    a. the local grocery stores

    b. the schools

    c. the parent/teacher organizations

    d. the local school boards

5. Sacrificing peanut butter and peanuts could save what?

    a. time

    b. money

    c. a child's life

    d. none of the above

ARTICLE FROM TIME FOR KIDS

Name_____ Date_____

Lesson 10

Whole-Story Comprehension

Directions: Read the story below and answer the questions on the following page.

Peanut Problems

Some kids are allergic to peanuts. Should schools be nut-free zones? When Nicholas Pave was three-years-old, he ate a piece of brownie at a party. Within seconds, his throat was itching and his nose was running. An hour later, he started throwing up. Says Nicholas now: "It was scary."

How can one bite of one brownie make someone so sick? Nicholas was having an allergic reaction to peanut-butter chips in the brownie. His mom quickly called the doctor and gave Nicholas some medicine. Without the medicine, he might have stopped breathing. Some people allergic to peanuts have died after eating them.

People who are allergic to peanuts must avoid anything containing a peanut or its oil. Sometimes just smelling or touching peanut oil or peanut dust causes an allergic reaction. That can turn a school cafeteria into a danger zone!

Now some schools have decided not to take any chances. They're cracking down on peanut products to protect allergic kids. In some school cafeterias, peanut-free tables are being set aside. In other schools, no one is allowed to bring any "peanutty" foods at all.

Banning peanut butter creates some sticky problems. Peanut-butter-and-jelly sandwiches are popular. They are a nutritious, affordable food for most families. However, there are many choices for a healthful lunch. School cafeterias can provide a wide choice of foods that are safe for all kids. They can even send home suggestions for bag lunches that don't include peanuts. People should be willing to sacrifice a particular food if it might save a child's life. All schools should ban peanuts and peanut products.

Even if all schools don't ban peanuts, Ann Munoz-Furlong of the Food Allergy Network points out that teachers and students should have an emergency plan to deal with any allergy attack. Allergic kids should always wash their hands before eating and should never trade foods with other kids. Kids should feel safe in the classroom and the cafeteria.

Level 4   Lesson 10

Name_____ Date_____

Whole-Story Comprehension *(cont.)*

Directions: After you have read the story on the previous page, answer the questions below.

1. What symptoms did Nicholas have that indicated he had an allergy?
   a. His hands were sweaty.
   b. He began running a fever.
   c. He had an itchy throat and hives.
   d. He had an itchy throat, a runny nose, and began throwing up.

2. Without medicine, what could have happened to Nicholas?
   a. He could have eaten too many peanuts.
   b. He could have thrown up his food.
   c. He could have stopped breathing or even died.
   d. He could have eaten more brownies.

3. In some schools, students are not allowed to bring what types of foods?
   a. "peanutty" foods
   b. foods that have walnuts
   c. video games
   d. popcorn and peanuts

4. Other than just peanuts, what else can cause an allergic reaction?
   a. smelling or touching peanut oil or peanut dust
   b. dust mites
   c. peanuts and walnuts
   d. none of the above

5. What are some schools doing as a result of peanut allergies?
   a. sending home suggestions for students with allergies
   b. enlisting volunteers to watch for allergic students
   c. banning "peanutty" products
   d. serving a choice of brownies with peanuts or without peanuts

6. Which of the following statements is an opinion?
   a. People can be allergic to peanuts.
   b. Schools should ban all peanut products.
   c. Peanut-butter-and-jelly sandwiches are nutritious.
   d. People allergic to peanuts should avoid peanut oil as well.

7. The Food Allergy Network suggests that teachers should be prepared with
   a. an emergency plan in case someone has an allergic reaction.
   b. plenty of peanut butter.
   c. a list of suggestions for different types of sandwiches.
   d. information to give parents about allergies.

8. What tips should students with peanut allergies remember?
   a. Eat all of your lunch.
   b. Drink milk with sandwiches.
   c. Share food with only people you know.
   d. Wash hands before eating and never trade food.

Enrichment

Directions: Read the information below and use it to answer the following questions.

In the article about peanuts, there were many signal words. What are signal words? Signal words are used to connect ideas together. There are many types of signal words, and you probably already use them in your writing without knowing it. Look at the types of signal words below. The italicized words came from the article.

For example:

because	but	despite	*however*
so that	similar to	too	next
resulting from	later	lately	until
within	once	also	*though*
inside	*now*	and finally	even
so	although	more	

Signal words are used to help us understand what we read. Signal words help us understand how the information is organized and to provide clues about what is important. They help us anticipate the direction of a piece of writing. They tell us that there are more ideas to come, that there is an order to ideas, and that there is going to be a change of direction. They may also tell us where and when something is happening or give something emphasis. They prepare us for examples and tell us that a condition or modification is coming up. Signal words are independent of the content; they can be used with any piece of writing.

Select the correct signal word from the box to fill in the sentences. Some of the signal words may be used more than once, or not at all.

1. Some children are allergic to peanuts, _____ though they don't know it.

2. _____ of the danger to students, some schools are banning peanut products.

3. _____ the cafeteria has agreed to send home ideas for sack lunches, some parents are still very unhappy!

4. Scientists have _____ found that peanut oil and dust should also be avoided.

5. _____, schools should have an emergency plan for allergy attacks.

Level 4　　　　　　　　　　　　　　　　　　　　　　　　　　　　Lesson 10

Name_____　Date_____

Graphic Development

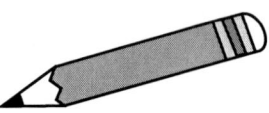

Directions: Read the following information and then use the fictitious picture graph below to answer the questions about kids with allergies.

> One in 20 kids has a food allergy. There are many food allergies, but there are other types of allergies as well. Some of these nonfood allergies include dust, pollen, lotions, and perfumes. An allergy is when the "body thinks that a substance is a harmful invader and tries to attack it."
>
> **Kids with Allergies at Hualapai Elementary School**
>
> | | |
> |---|---|
> | Milk allergy | ☺ ☺ ☺ ☺ ☺ ☺ ☺ |
> | Shellfish allergy | ☺ ☺ ☺ ☺ |
> | Pollen allergy | ☺ ☺ |
> | Nut allergy | ☺ ☺ ☺ ☺ ☺ |
> | Wheat or soy allergy | ☺ ☺ ☺ |
>
> ☺ = 5 students

1. What allergy do the most people in this graph have?
   _____

2. How many more people have an allergy to nuts compared to people with an allergy to shellfish?
   _____

3. What is the title of this graph?
   _____

4. Which type of allergy on this chart has nothing to do with what a person eats?
   _____

5. How many people are allergic to milk?
   _____

Sentence Comprehension

Directions: Read the following sentence carefully and answer the questions below "True" (T) or "False" (F).

> When large numbers of people began settling in Florida nearly a hundred years ago, the Everglades were considered a worthless swampland.

1. The large number of people settling in Florida helped to sustain the swampland. _____
2. The Everglades were thought to be worthless swampland. _____
3. Over a hundred years ago, people came and settled in the Everglades. _____
4. The Everglades are located in Oklahoma. _____
5. The Everglades didn't exist 100 years ago. _____

Word Study

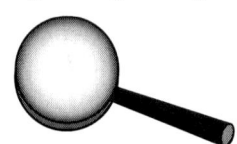

Directions: Look below at the chart showing the meaning of the different word parts. Find the meaning of each word by combining the meanings of its parts from the chart.

> *Ecosystem* is a word that is a combination of two words. The first part, *eco-*, means *habitat* or *environment*. *System* means *interdependent group of items forming a unified whole*. Combining the two parts makes the word *ecosystem* which means *the complex of a community and its environment functioning as an ecological unit in nature*.

Word	Prefix	Word Root	Suffix
dismissal	dis- "apart"	-mis- "to send"	-al "action"
complicate	com- "together"	-plic- "fold"	-ate "to make"
emotion	e- "out"	-mot- "to move"	-ion "state"
incredible	in- "not"	-cred- "to believe"	-ible "capable"
composer	com- "together"	-pos- "to place"	-er "a doer"
duplexity	du- "two"	-plex- "fold"	-ity "condition"
resonance	re- "again"	-son- "to sound"	-ance "condition"

1. commotion _____
2. mission _____
3. composer _____
4. emotional _____
5. expose _____

Paragraph Comprehension

Directions: Read the paragraph below and answer the following questions.

> But a closer look reveals a busy, buzzing natural world. Hundreds of species make up the Everglades' ecosystem. Egrets and white ibis soar above the water. Lime-green tree frogs croak. Craggy alligators lurk below the swamp's surface.

1. The Everglades contain hundreds of
   a. birds.
   b. frogs.
   c. species.
   d. alligators.

2. What are egrets and white ibis?
   a. reindeer
   b. extinct animals
   c. birds
   d. insects

3. The word craggy probably means
   a. rough and rugged.
   b. kind and considerate.
   c. patient and loving.
   d. calm and peaceful.

4. What lurks below the swamp?
   a. eel
   b. sharks
   c. crocodiles
   d. alligators

5. What color are the tree frogs?
   a. chartreuse
   b. lime-green
   c. dark green
   d. light green

Whole-Story Comprehension

Directions: Read the story below and answer the questions on the following page.

Looking Out for the Gators

Florida's Everglades National Park doesn't look like much from an airplane. A flat, soggy field of tall grass stretches toward the horizon. A few trees dot the landscape under the hot Florida sun.

But a closer look reveals a busy, buzzing natural world. Hundreds of species make up the Everglades' ecosystem. Egrets and white ibis soar above the water. Lime-green tree frogs croak. Craggy alligators lurk below the swamp's surface. Now, after years of bad planning, this habitat may be dying. Dozens of its species are endangered.

When large numbers of people began settling in Florida nearly a hundred years ago, the Everglades were considered a worthless swampland. Builders did their best to drain the swamp. Farms and cities sprang up where alligators once roamed freely.

In the 1920s, Army engineers straightened rivers and built canals and dikes to prevent flooding and keep water supplies stable for farms and cities. They didn't realize that changing the flow of water would harm the ecosystem drastically. The Everglades, which once covered 4,000 square miles, shrank by half. Populations of birds, alligators, and other animals shrank, too.

"Everything depends on the water," explains Sandy Dayhoff, education coordinator for Everglades National Park, "not only having enough water, but the right amount at the right time." Dayhoff compares the Everglades with a giant bathtub. In the rainy season, the tub is full. In the dry season, it slowly drains. Human activities are interfering with both parts of this natural cycle.

Farmers, especially sugar-cane growers, have created another problem. A chemical called phosphorus is found in crop fertilizers and animal wastes. Sugar-cane plantations and dairy farms dump tons of phosphorus into South Florida's waters every year.

Some plants absorb it better than others. Cattails, for example, are great at absorbing phosphorus. This plant is beginning to take over the park, crowding out native saw grass, which many animals need.

In the 1980s, people began to realize the Everglades were in trouble. Engineers are now trying to put rivers back on their old winding courses. It won't be cheap. The plan will cost $1.5 billion over seven years. Some say sugar-cane growers must pay their fair share. One idea is to add a tax on sugar that would help pay for the plan. But sugar growers say a tax would hurt their business and risk the jobs of 40,000 sugar workers.

Still, nearly everyone agrees that the Everglades must be rescued. "There's no other place like this on Earth," says Dayhoff. "It would be terrible to destroy a national treasure like this."

Whole Story Comprehension (cont.)

Directions: After you have read the story on the previous page, answer the questions below.

1. What happened in the 1920s?
   a. Army engineers straightened rivers and built canals to prevent flooding.
   b. Hundreds and thousands of animals immediately became extinct.
   c. The swamp was closed down.
   d. Builders began requesting permits to reinstate animals on the endangered species list.

2. To what does Sandy Dayhoff compare the Everglades?
   a. a large lake
   b. the Atlantic Ocean
   c. a bathtub
   d. swamps in South America

3. What change affected the ecosystem?
   a. the amount of species in the Everglades
   b. the flow of water in the Everglades
   c. the amount of homes being built in the Everglades
   d. the number of animals located in the Everglades

4. The Everglades once covered how many square miles?
   a. 3,000
   b. 7,000
   c. 6,000
   d. 4,000

5. What type of growers have created another problem?
   a. sugar-cane growers
   b. wheat growers
   c. cotton growers
   d. orange growers

6. What problem does the chemical phosphorus cause?
   a. It causes all the plants to die.
   b. Cattails absorb this chemical faster than other plants, and they are starting to take over.
   c. The chemical gets in the food we eat.
   d. The chemical is leaving the land barren and so more crops can't be grown.

7. When did people begin to realize the Everglades were in trouble?
   a. 1920s
   b. 1960s
   c. 1970s
   d. 1980s

8. What is the plan that has been suggested to correct the problem?
   a. to take all the endangered animals out and transfer them to parks in the area
   b. to create new crops to take the place of the sugar crops
   c. to recreate the Everglades ecosystem somewhere else
   d. to put the rivers back on their old winding courses

Enrichment

Directions: Read the following information and use it to complete the sentences below.

> "A flat, soggy field of tall grass stretches toward the horizon."
>
> "... a closer look reveals a busy, buzzing natural world."
>
> "A few trees dot the landscape under the hot Florida sun."
>
> The author of "Looking Out for the Gators," selected colorful words to help paint the picture of the Everglades in Florida's National Park. Descriptive language usually comes from adjectives and adverbs. Adjectives describe nouns, and adverbs describe verbs. Adverbs and adjectives can be powerful descriptive words in your writing, if used correctly. Look at how the adjectives and adverbs create more descriptive sentences below.
>
> 1. The *healthy, adorable* baby cooed *happily* into her mother's ear.
>
> 2. The *excited* couple *quickly* jumped into their limousine.
>
> 3. The *screaming* and *shouting* fans *hastily* lunged at the *famous* singer.

Practice using adverbs and adjectives by rewriting the sentences below. Select adjectives and adverbs from the word lists to add more detail to the sentences.

List of Adverbs	List of Adjectives
happily	ferocious
angrily	magnificent
hastily	grand
sadly	craggy
lovingly	beautiful

1. The alligator swam.

_____

2. Hundreds of species were dying.

_____

3. The white ibis flew.

_____

4. Builders tore up the landscape.

_____

5. The scientist was sad about the result of the chemicals.

_____

Level 4											Lesson 11

Name_____ Date_____

Graphic Development

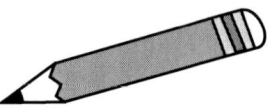

Directions: Read the following information and then use the fictional time line below to answer the questions.

The Everglades National Park is one of a kind. There is no other place like it on the earth. People have learned the damage that chemicals and years of bad planning have done to this fragile ecosystem. What will the years ahead hold in store for the Everglades?

Trouble in the Everglades

2000s	Animals in the Everglades are on the endangered list.
1980s	People begin to realize the Everglades are in trouble.
1960s	Farmers begin using phosphorus, which affects the Everglades.
1940s	Building continues in the Everglades.
1920s	Army engineers straighten rivers and build canals.
1900s	Large numbers of people begin settling in Florida.

1. What did army engineers do in the 1920s?
_____

2. In what decade did people begin to realize that the Everglades were in trouble?
_____

3. What is the title of this time line?
_____

4. What happened in the 1900s to the Everglades?
_____

5. What is the name of the chemical being used in the 60s and 70s?
_____

86   #10334 Nonfiction Comprehension Test Practice   ©Shell Educational Publishing

Level 4

Lesson 12

Name_____ Date_____

Sentence Comprehension

Directions: Read the following sentence carefully and answer the questions below "True" (T) or "False" (F).

> But it is now possible to buy for two dollars Beanie Babies that originally sold for five dollars.

1. A Beanie Baby can change in price. ____
2. The price of a Beanie Baby can decrease. ____
3. Beanie Babies originally sold for five dollars. ____
4. It is impossible to buy a Beanie Baby for less than five dollars. ____
5. A Beanie Baby never sells for less than the original price. ____

Word Study

Directions: Match the words in Column A with their synonyms in Column B. The first one has been done for you.

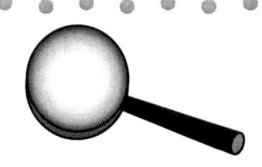

urgent

The meaning of *urgent* is *calling for immediate attention*. A word that has a similar meaning to urgent is the word pressing. Synonyms are words that have similar meanings. Synonyms are used in dictionaries to define words.

Column A	Column B
1. add	make, construct
2. ask	under, below
3. bad	join, unite, combine
4. beneath	bring, lug, transport
5. bold	summon, command
6. brilliant	naughty, evil, wicked
7. call	bright, radiant
8. build	youngsters, kids
9. carry	question, inquire
10. children	valiant, brave, daring

©Shell Educational Publishing   #10334 Nonfiction Comprehension Test Practice

Level 4   Lesson 12

Name_____ Date_____

Paragraph Comprehension

Directions: Read the paragraph below and answer the following questions.

> That lower pricing does not apply to the Ty Beanie Baby Billionaire Bear. The first Billionaire Bear was produced in 1998 when it was presented to Ty, Inc. employees at a company party. That Bear, now "retired," can be purchased for $350. Number two, given to employees in 1999, has a much higher price tag: $1,500–$1,600. Only 612 Billionaire Bear number 7s were released to employees in 2004; the number 7 price tag is $500. (Caution: Prices subject to change.)

1. The first owners of the Billionaire Bears are

     a. H. Ty Warner and his family.
     b. Ty, Inc. employees.
     c. the highest bidders.
     d. American billionaires.

2. The first Billionaire Bear was produced in

     a. 2004.
     b. 1989.
     c. 1998.
     d. 1994.

3. Number two Billionaire Bear

     a. costs more than number one.
     b. costs more than number seven.
     c. costs more than when first issued.
     d. costs less than when first issued.

4. The prices quoted in the paragraph

     a. will never change.
     b. could change anytime.
     c. will increase every day.
     d. will decrease every day.

5. If a Ty employee sold his 1998 Billionaire Bear for $700,

     a. the seller's profit would be 25 percent.
     b. the seller's profit would be 50 percent.
     c. the seller's profit would be 75 percent.
     d. the seller's profit would be 100 percent.

ARTICLE FROM TIME FOR KIDS

Name_____ Date_____

Lesson 12

Whole-Story Comprehension

Directions: Read the story below and answer the questions on the following page.

Bye-Bye, Beanies?

December 31, 1999, was the end of the millennium. Would it be the end of Beanie Babies, too? In September 1999, Ty, Inc., the maker of Beanie Babies, posted this urgent message on its Web site: "Very Important Notice: On December 31, 1999 . . . all Beanies will be retired."

H. Ty Warner, creator and manufacturer of Beanie Babies responded to the uproar his notice caused. The next message on the Ty, Inc. Web site announced that anyone could vote on December 31, 1999, to decide whether the company should continue to produce Beanie Babies. The vote was 91 percent in favor of more of the plush toys.

More there have been. Several new kinds of Beanie Babies were introduced: Beanie Kids, Baby Ty, Jingle Babies, Beanie Boppers, Basket Beanies, and more. A Beanie Baby of some Beanie category is offered for every holiday and just about every widely known event. That includes holidays and events in other countries as well as the United States.

Though the collection craze is not as great as it was in the earlier Beanie Baby years, 1994–1999, Beanie Babies are still being collected, sold, and traded. But it is now possible to buy for two dollars Beanie Babies that originally sold for five dollars. Quite a change!

That lower pricing does not apply to the Ty Beanie Baby Billionaire Bear. The first Billionaire Bear was produced in 1998 when it was presented to Ty employees at a company party. That Bear, now "retired," can be purchased for $350. Number two, given to employees in 1999, has a much higher price tag: $1,500–$1,600. Only 612 Billionaire Bear number 7s were released to employees in 2004; the number 7 price tag is $500. (Caution: Prices subject to change.)

Each month a certain number of Beanies is retired and a variety of new releases is announced, as many as 10 each month. Meanwhile, in July 2004, McDonalds restarted the Teenie Beanie Giveaways to celebrate the 25th anniversary of the Happy Meal, giving away 12 Teenie Beanies.

Perhaps there will be an announcement someday that the end of Beanie Babies is coming soon. Until then, anyone can go to the Ty Web site and post on the Ty Talk Cyberboard an idea or two for new Beanies. Suggestions include a Havanese dog, a goldfinch, and a Himalayan cat. Warner began his plush toy business in 1985, selling a stuffed Himalayan cat in 10 different colors, filling orders from his condo.

In a relatively short time, Warner needed warehouse space and employees. In 1993, Beanie Babies were born. Instead of "Bye-Bye," customers seem plentiful and are saying "More, more."

Level 4   Lesson 12

Name_____ Date_____

Whole-Story Comprehension *(cont.)*

Directions: After you have read the story on the previous page answer the questions below.

1. What did the announcement in December 1999 say?

   a. a new line of Beanies would be introduced
   b. all the Beanies would be retired
   c. the price of Beanies would be going up
   d. the supply of Beanies would be greater than last year

2. Beanie Baby customers voted to

   a. discontinue the toys in 1999.
   b. discontinue the toys in 2000.
   c. continue the toys until 2000.
   d. continue the toys.

3. It is possible to buy Beanie Babies for

   a. Christmas.
   b. Halloween.
   c. Easter.
   d. all of the above.

4. How are the prices set for the Billionaire Bears?

   a. Ty sets the price for each at $100.
   b. Children ages ten to twelve set the prices.
   c. Prices vary and may change at any time.
   d. Each state's governor sets the prices.

5. How many Beanie Babies are retired each month?

   a. more than 15
   b. 5
   c. 25
   d. as many as 10

6. How many different types of Beanie Babies did McDonalds give away to celebrate the 25th anniversary of the Happy Meal?

   a. half a dozen
   b. a gross
   c. one dozen
   d. a baker's dozen

7. Why is it significant that a customer wants a Himalayan cat Beanie?

   a. Everyone knows Himalayan cats are ugly.
   b. Before Beanies, Ty sold stuffed Himalayan cats.
   c. Himalayan cats are very popular.
   d. Cats cannot be Beanie Babies.

8. When were Beanie Babies "born"?

   a. 2000
   b. 1999
   c. 1993
   d. 2001

Level 4   Lesson 12

Name_____ Date_____

Enrichment

Directions: Read the information below and use it to find the plural form of the words that follow.

> Spelling errors commonly occur when the writer changes a singular noun to a plural noun. Most plural words have an **s** added to them to become plural. There are many words where the spelling of the word changes by making it plural. Look at the following plural rules:
>
> - Add an **s** to most nouns to make them plural.
> - Nouns ending with a consonant and a **y** change the **y** to **i** and add **es**.
> - Nouns that end in **ch**, **sh**, **ss**, **s**, **x**, **o**, *or* **s** add **es**. If the word ends in **f** or **fe**, you would usually change to **v** and then add **es**.
> - Some words do not add endings, but change their form altogether. (For example: man—men, ox—oxen)
> - Some words keep the same spelling in the plural form.

What is the plural form of each of these words? Some of these words are taken directly from the Beanie Baby article.

1. sale _____
2. suspect _____
3. address _____
4. Beanie _____
5. bean _____
6. potato _____
7. leaf _____
8. deer _____
9. worry _____
10. bunch _____
11. tooth _____
12. collector _____
13. mess _____
14. company _____
15. inch _____
16. coach _____
17. belief _____
18. thief _____

Level 4   Lesson 12

Name_____ Date_____

Graphic Development

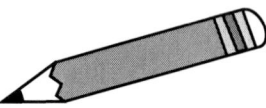

Directions: Read the following information and use the line graph to answer the questions below.

Were Beanie Babies really gone? The startling news in December of 1999 left Beanie Baby collectors worried. The price and value of Beanies grew each time they were "retired" and no longer made. Customers thought that the announcement was meant to drive customers to buy Beanies. What were the sales of Beanies like?

The Rise and Fall of Beanies

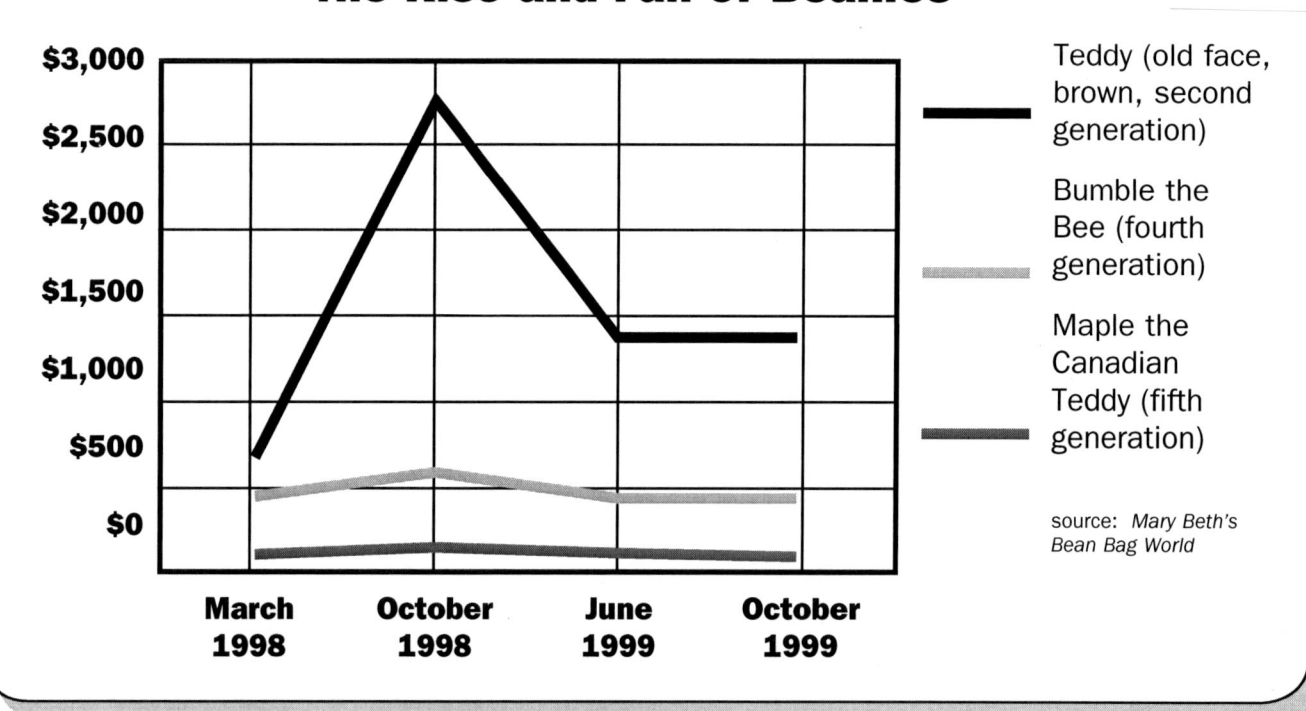

Legend:
— Teddy (old face, brown, second generation)
— Bumble the Bee (fourth generation)
— Maple the Canadian Teddy (fifth generation)

source: *Mary Beth's Bean Bag World*

X-axis: March 1998, October 1998, June 1999, October 1999
Y-axis: $0 to $3,000

1. In what year was the most amount of money spent on Beanies?
   _____

2. Of the three Beanies displayed on this graph, which Beanie was purchased the most?
   _____

3. What is the source of information for this graph?
   _____

4. What is the title of this graph?
   _____

5. How much more profit did Teddy make than Bumble the Bee in October 1999?
   _____

Level 4   Lesson 13

Name_____ Date_____

Sentence Comprehension

Directions: Read the following sentence carefully and answer the questions below "True" (T) or "False" (F).

> Checketts, who calls himself a "high-thrill junkie," climbed to the very top of the 300-foot Power Tower soon after it was built.

1. Checketts is a high-thrill junkie. _____
2. Checketts was injured when he fell 300 feet. _____
3. Checketts climbed to the top of Power Tower before it was finished. _____
4. Checketts probably likes adventure. _____
5. This sentence is about all the amusement park rides in Las Vegas, Nevada. _____

Word Study

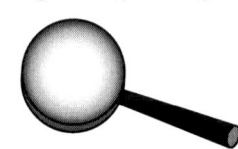

Directions: Select one of the following suffixes to add to one of the words below.

> **sickness**
>
> *Sickness* is an illness or a weakened condition. The *suffix* in sickness is *ness*. A suffix comes at the end of a word. A suffix can tell you what type of word it is part of and how it should be used in a sentence.

| EN (made of, make) | NESS (with) | ATE (cause, make) |
| AL (relating to) | ABLE, IBLE (able, can do) | SHIP (quality, skill) |

1. nature + _____ = _____
2. weak + _____ = _____
3. friend + _____ = _____
4. careless + _____ = _____
5. agree + _____ = _____

©Shell Educational Publishing   #10334 Nonfiction Comprehension Test Practice

Level 4   Lesson 13

Name_____   Date_____

Paragraph Comprehension

Directions: Read the paragraph below and answer the following questions.

> "My job is a blast, literally," says Stan Checketts of Logan, Utah. Checketts gets paid to give people thrills and chills! He invents amusement park rides. "It's great for people to scream and smile and have a great rush," says Checketts, president of S&S Sports Power, Inc. His scream machine, Power Tower, at Cedar Point Amusement Park in Sandusky, Ohio, is the world's tallest tower ride. Riders shoot 240 feet up two of the ride's towers at the same time while the other riders drop down the other two towers. A strong blast of air pushes them all along at 50 miles an hour. The ride takes just three seconds each way.

1. Checketts gets paid to

   a. climb his amusement rides.

   b. warn people of amusement ride dangers.

   c. give people thrills and chills on amusement park rides.

   d. invent new amusement video games.

2. The name of Checketts' scream machine at Cedar Point is

   a. Tower of Terror.

   b. Power Plus.

   c. Cedar Point Terror.

   d. Power Tower.

3. The Power Tower is

   a. the first tower ever built.

   b. over its budget.

   c. the smallest tower ride in the world.

   d. the world's tallest tower ride.

4. What shoots people up at 50 mph?

   a. air

   b. water

   c. energy

   d. electricity

5. The ride takes only

   a. passengers that are four feet and under.

   b. three seconds each way.

   c. children.

   d. tickets.

Lesson 13

Name_____ Date_____

Whole-Story Comprehension

Directions: Read the story below and answer the questions on the following page.

Tower of Thrills

"My job is a blast, literally," says Stan Checketts of Logan, Utah. Checketts gets paid to give people thrills and chills! He invents amusement park rides. "It's great for people to scream and smile and have a great rush," says Checketts, president of S&S Sports Power, Inc. His scream machine, Power Tower, at Cedar Point Amusement Park in Sandusky, Ohio, is the world's tallest tower ride. Riders shoot 240 feet up two of the ride's towers at the same time while other riders drop down the other two towers. A strong blast of air pushes them along at 50 miles an hour. The ride takes just three seconds each way.

Checketts, who calls himself a "high-thrill junkie," climbed to the very top of the 300-foot Power Tower soon after it was built! He climbs all of his tallest creations. He even hiked up Big Shot, the tower ride he built on top of the fifth tallest building in the U.S., the Stratosphere Hotel in Las Vegas, Nevada.

Playing with kids inspired Checketts to build thrill rides like the Power Tower. "The concept evolved from tossing my nine children in the air when they were little," Checketts said. Now his eight grandchildren can get a high-speed rush on his rides. What do they think of his job? "They think Grandpa's crazy," laughs Checketts, who also bungee jumps, skydives, and climbs mountains.

There is one thing the brave Checketts can't stomach. Longer thrill rides, including many roller coasters, give him motion sickness! "Usually nobody gets sick on my rides," he says, "because they happen so quickly."

What will Checketts do now that he has built a record-breaking thrill ride? "There are still a lot of crazy ideas in my head for high-thrill rides," he says. Next: an air-powered roller coaster. Sounds like a blast!

Level 4   Lesson 13

Name_____   Date_____

Whole-Story Comprehension *(cont.)*

Directions: After you have read the story on the previous page, answer the questions below.

1. A "high-thrill" junkie is someone who
   a. eats too much junk food.
   b. likes to do adventurous things.
   c. is addicted to drugs.
   d. is afraid of amusement parks.

2. What does Checketts do on all of his tall creations?
   a. climbs them
   b. jumps off of them
   c. enjoys taking pictures of them
   d. advertises them

3. What is the inspiration behind these tower rides?
   a. when Checketts rode on an airplane
   b. Checketts saw them in a movie
   c. the thrill of riding
   d. when Checketts used to toss his children in the air

4. Checketts' grandchildren think he is
   a. strong.
   b. brave.
   c. crazy.
   d. fun.

5. Which statement is an opinion?
   a. Checkett invents amusement park rides.
   b. Roller coasters give Checketts motion sickness.
   c. Checketts is a brave and exciting person.
   d. Checketts plans to build an air-powered roller coaster.

6. What other interests does Checketts have?
   a. bungee jumping, roller blading, and rappelling
   b. bungee jumping, skydiving, and mountain climbing
   c. cooking, rappelling, and mountain climbing
   d. mountain climbing and rappelling

7. Checketts is President of
   a. Amusements, Inc.
   b. S&S Sports Power, Inc.
   c. Sports and Power, Inc.
   d. S&S Power Towers, Inc.

8. Where did Checketts build the ride Big Shot?
   a. In Chicago at the World Fair
   b. In New York City
   c. Atop the Stratosphere Hotel in Las Vegas
   d. On the fifth tallest building in Laughlin, Nevada

Enrichment

Directions: Read the information below and use it to answer the following questions.

The way you begin your writing will either leave the reader engaged or uninterested. There are many ways to capture the attention of the reader. Listed below are descriptions of leads that can be used to begin a piece of writing.

1. **Personal Experience**—Using personal experience gives the reader a chance to know you a little bit better. People can often relate to a personal experience and it helps connect with what you are writing about.
2. **Strong Visual Image**—Painting a picture for the readers captures their interest and helps them visualize what you are talking about. Visual images can create a lasting impression.
3. **Rhetorical Question**—A rhetorical question is a question you ask at the beginning to get the reader thinking. You never expect the reader to answer the question.
4. **Facts and Statistics**—Using facts and statistics can be a powerful tool, especially if the facts and statistics are amazing or disturbing. Facts and statistics can set the record straight from the beginning and can help establish validity for the topic being read.
5. **Dialogue/Quotation**—Using dialogue or a quote will entice the reader. Quotes and dialogues allow the reader to see what other people think about the subject. This gives you a chance to support your claims.

Place a number next to each sentence corresponding to the type of lead that has been used in the following beginnings. The first one has been done for you. The first one is also the same lead used in the actual article, "Tower of Thrills."

___5___ "My job is a blast, literally," says Stan Checketts of Logan, Utah. Checketts gets paid to give people thrills and chills! He invents amusement park rides.

_____ I remember the first time I ever rode on the Power Tower with my mother. The look of desperation and panic on her face will never leave my mind. I remember my mind screaming as we came flying down. I knew I was going to hear about this ride. Stan Checketts would like to hear about it too. Checketts invents amusement park rides for a living.

_____ Seventy-five percent of all people attending amusement parks enjoy the tallest rides the most. Only eighteen percent of all amusement parks have tall rides. Based on these statistics, Stan Checketts has a big job ahead of him. He invents amusement park rides.

_____ Think back to a time when you were on a roller coaster ride. Picture the look that must have been in your eyes. Imagine what you were thinking at the time. Imagine what you would tell the person who invented the ride. Stan Checketts just might be that person. Checketts invents amusement park rides for a living.

_____ How did it feel the last time you dropped 240 feet? Can you remember the adrenaline rush you had as you came screaming downward? Do wish you could have that experience again and again? Stan Checketts hopes that you do. Checketts invents amusement park rides.

Level 4 Lesson 13

Name_____ Date_____

Graphic Development

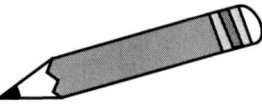

Directions: Read the following information and use the pictograph to answer the questions below.

> Swoosh! What a thrill! What is your favorite amusement park ride? Amusement parks dot the United States and bring thrills and chills to kids and adults alike. The graph below shows the favorite amusement park rides of students in Mrs. Johnson's fourth-grade class.
>
> **Favorite Rides in Mrs. Johnson's Class**
>
> | Ride | Stars |
> |---|---|
> | **Power Tower** | ☆ ☆ ☆ ☆ ☆ ☆ ☆ ☆ |
> | **Merry-Go-Round** | ☆ ☆ ☆ ☆ |
> | **Roller Coaster** | ☆ ☆ ☆ ☆ ☆ |
> | **Big Shot** | ☆ ☆ ☆ ☆ ☆ |
> | **Tea Cups** | ☆ ☆ ☆ |
>
> ☆ = 1 student

1. What does each star represent?

_____

2. How many people chose the Power Tower as their favorite ride?

_____

3. What ride was chosen the least by the students?

_____

4. How many students' responses are shown on the pictograph?

_____

5. Which amusement ride was chosen by ten students?

_____

98   #10334 Nonfiction Comprehension Test Practice   ©Shell Educational Publishing

Level 4   Lesson 14

Name_____   Date_____

Sentence Comprehension

Directions: Read the following sentence carefully and answer the questions below "True" (T) or "False" (F).

> Rangers tried to control the growth by slaughtering older elephants and then moving the young elephants to other parks and reserves.

1. There was a growth problem with the elephants. _____
2. The younger elephants were slaughtered. _____
3. The rangers had to train older elephants. _____
4. Families of elephants were divided up. _____
5. The young elephants were moved to other parks. _____

Word Study

Directions: Match the pronunciations in Column A with the correct word in Column B.

Hluhluwe-Umfolozi

What?! That is a hard word to pronounce. Fortunately, there is a pronunciation included for this word. Hluhluwe-Umfolozi [Slush-looey Oom-fall-o-zee] is a park in southeastern South Africa. The pronunciation of each word can be found in a dictionary. The pronunciation is found immediately following the word. You will find the pronunciation key in the bottom right corner of each dictionary page.

Column A	Column B
1. \spär′ kel\	spat
2. \spăt\	sparrow
3. \spēk\	spark
4. \spärk\	sparkle
5. \spăr′ō\	speak

©Shell Educational Publishing   #10334 Nonfiction Comprehension Test Practice

Level 4   Lesson 14

Name_____   Date_____

Paragraph Comprehension

Directions: Read the paragraph below and answer the following questions.

> "The whole thing has much to do with the setup of elephant society," says South African zoologist Marian Garai. Elephants normally live in tight-knit groups. Older males keep young bulls in line. But no such role models were provided for the orphans from Kruger. Garai believes this upset the young elephants and led them to lash out at rhinos.

1. How do older bulls help younger bulls?

   a. They show them how to hunt.
   b. They keep younger bulls in line.
   c. They demonstrate how to eat.
   d. They carry them over rough terrain.

2. In which country is the problem with the elephants?

   a. Namibia
   b. Botswana
   c. Zimbabwe
   d. South Africa

3. What are the orphans at Kruger lacking?

   a. enough nutrients in their diet
   b. safe surroundings in which to live
   c. older elephants as role models
   d. their mothers

4. What did the elephants do to the rhinos?

   a. They lashed out at some of the rhinos.
   b. They included them in their family groups.
   c. They have taken over their territory.
   d. They have protected the rhinos.

5. Elephants normally

   a. live in clans.
   b. live in tight-knit groups.
   c. eat plants and vegetables.
   d. fight each other.

Whole-Story Comprehension

Directions: Read the story below and answer the questions on the following page.

Bullies in the Park!

The trouble started some years ago. Nearly every month, rangers in Pilanesberg National Park in northwestern South Africa would find an endangered white rhinoceros that had been killed. Then the same thing started happening at another park in southeastern South Africa.

Rhinos are sometimes hunted for their valuable horns. But no one had touched the horns of these animals. Their wounds hadn't come from guns.

The rangers who solved the crime were surprised to learn what was to blame. Young male elephants behaved badly because they had grown up without the attention of caring adults.

Several years ago, the population of elephants in South Africa's Kruger National Park was growing too large. Rangers tried to control the growth by slaughtering older elephants and then moving the younger elephants to other parks and reserves. Since 1976, almost 1,500 orphans—600 of them males, or bulls—have been moved to unfamiliar locations, where they grew up without older elephants around them.

Moving the orphans helped preserve an endangered species. But it changed the elephants' social order.

"The whole thing has much to do with the setup of elephant society," says South African zoologist Marian Garai. Elephants normally live in tight-knit groups. Older males keep young bulls in line. But no such role models were provided for the orphans from Kruger. Garai believes this upset the young elephants and led them to lash out at rhinos.

"Elephants are complex and intelligent creatures," explains Garai. "They aren't immune to stress."

What can be done? Some rangers believe the elephant bullies need foster parents. When two adult female circus elephants were returned to Pilanesberg in 1979, the nervous orphans settled down.

Now officials hope a similar plan will work for the rhino-bashing bulls. Kruger Park will move entire families of elephants to new homes instead of killing the elders and hauling away their young, and a few 40-year-old male elephants will be moved to Pilanesberg.

Preserving families may be the key to raising well-behaved elephants. Meanwhile, South Africa's white rhinos had better watch out.

Level 4   **Lesson 14**

Name_____ Date_____

Whole-Story Comprehension (cont.)

Directions: After you have read the story on the previous page, answer the questions below.

1. When did the trouble with the rhinos begin?
    a. five years ago
    b. some years ago
    c. fifteen years ago
    d. a little over a year ago

2. Exactly what was the problem at the park in South Africa?
    a. They were running out of food for the animals.
    b. They were having to shut down the park.
    c. They were unable to locate some of the elephants.
    d. They would periodically find white rhinos that had been killed.

3. The rangers were surprised
    a. to learn how easy it was to teach the elephants to behave.
    b. to learn the young male elephants were to blame.
    c. to learn that rhinos and elephants get along.
    d. to learn that the rivers were drying up in the park.

4. What did experts say the reason was for the angry elephants?
    a. They said it was because of the overcrowding.
    b. They said it was a result of not enough food.
    c. They said it was because there were no role models for the young elephants.
    d. They said it was because of the terrain in the parks.

5. Elephants are considered
    a. large and clumsy.
    b. creatures with low intelligence.
    c. complex and intelligent creatures.
    d. creatures with low immune deficiencies.

6. Since 1976,
    a. there have been 1,500 elephant orphans relocated.
    b. there have been 600 elephant orphans relocated.
    c. there have been 1,500 rhino attacks.
    d. there have been 1,978 rhino orphans.

7. What happened when the two circus elephants returned to Pilanesburg?
    a. The circus elephants had to be protected.
    b. The younger elephants became angry.
    c. The younger elephants settled down.
    d. The attacks on rhinos increased.

8. What do experts believe is the key to raising well-behaved elephants?
    a. provide circus elephants as role models
    b. preserve elephant families
    c. teach elephants self defense
    d. keep elephants separated

Level 4 Lesson 14

Name_____ Date_____

Enrichment

Directions: Read the information below and use it to answer the following questions.

> Have you ever thought of elephants as angry orphans? Have you thought of an elephant as a bully? Have you ever thought of an older elephant as a role model? The article, "Bullies in the Park," uses personification to make its point.
>
> Personification is a form of figurative language that gives an object, idea, or animal the characteristics of a person. Stating that an elephant is an orphan or a bully makes the elephant seem more like a person. Read the examples of personification below:
>
> - The cat marched her way to the front of the house.
> - The bird signaled the rest of the birds to sing at the same time.
> - The floor groaned as the cheerleaders jumped onto it.
> - The thought of becoming a teacher almost leaped out of my chest.

Circle only the sentences below that are examples of personification.

1. The sound of the alarm clock was shouting in my ear.
2. The elephant ate his food slowly.
3. The older elephant sat by the younger elephants.
4. The wind whispered through the trees of the jungle.
5. The tree stood firmly in its place.
6. Without adult attention, the elephants are suffering.
7. The rain drops danced on the leaves of the trees.
8. The elephant orphan angrily threw a fit.

©Shell Educational Publishing   #10334 Nonfiction Comprehension Test Practice   103

Level 4   Lesson 14

Name_____ Date_____

Graphic Development

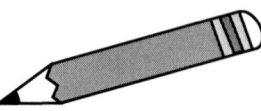

Directions: Read the following information and use the map below to answer the questions.

Elephants are intelligent and complex creatures. Do they have the capability of being so angry that they would kill a rhinoceros? Scientists are wrestling with these issues in parks in South Africa.

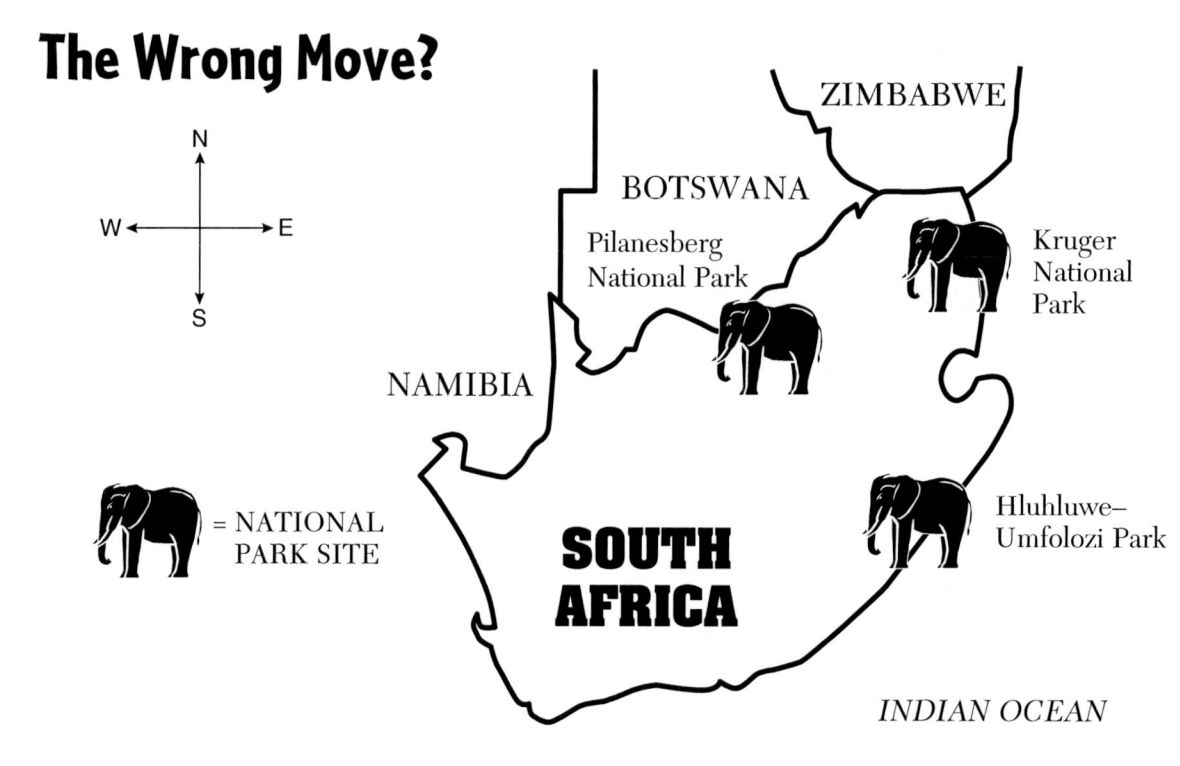

The Wrong Move?

(Map showing South Africa with neighboring countries Namibia, Botswana, and Zimbabwe. National park sites marked with elephant symbols: Pilanesberg National Park, Kruger National Park, Hluhluwe–Umfolozi Park. Indian Ocean to the southeast.)

1. How many national parks are located in South Africa?
   _____

2. What does the elephant symbol represent?
   _____

3. What is the title of this map?
   _____

4. What are the three countries that border South Africa?
   _____

5. Which park is located in the southeast of South Africa?
   _____

Level 4
Lesson 15

Name_____ Date_____

Sentence Comprehension

Directions: Read the following sentence carefully and answer the questions below "True" (T) or "False" (F).

> The police in Macon, Georgia, decided that a group of kids with a history of problems needed their own full-time cop.

1. The police decided a group of kids needed a cop. _____
2. The police officer arrested this group of kids. _____
3. The police officer is a full-time cop. _____
4. The kids in this neighborhood had a history of problems. _____
5. The police in Macon, Georgia, were giving up on this group of kids. _____

Word Study

Directions: Read the example in the box below and write the acronyms for the following organizations:

> **Y.E.S.**
>
> The acronym Y.E.S. stands for Youth Enrichment Services in the article about Officer Sinclair. An acronym is a word formed by the first letter of words in a phrase.

1. _____ Federal Bureau of Investigation
2. _____ Drug Abuse Resistance Education
3. _____ Central Intelligence Agency
4. _____ International Business Machines
5. _____ Internal Revenue Service
6. _____ National Aeronautics and Space Administration

©Shell Educational Publishing

Paragraph Comprehension

Directions: Read the paragraph below and answer the following questions.

> Each week, Officer Sinclair talks to the principal of Appling Middle School to check the students' grades and behavior. He meets with the kids twice a week and listens to them anytime they want to talk. In the summer, the group will go camping, tour a dairy farm, and perform service projects.

1. Each week, Officer Sinclair checks on the
   a. home life of each student.
   b. behavior and grades of the students.
   c. arrest reports of the students.
   d. amount of kids involved in after school programs.

2. What are some of the things the group will do in the summer?
   a. paint neighborhood houses
   b. go camping and roller blading
   c. tour a dairy farm and go rappelling
   d. go camping and tour a dairy farm

3. Officer Sinclair shows support by
   a. meeting with the kids twice a week to talk and listen.
   b. living in the students' homes.
   c. teaching at the school.
   d. preparing the students for police training.

4. The students attend
   a. a private school.
   b. Appling High School.
   c. Appling Middle School.
   d. Appling Charter School.

5. Students will have an opportunity to
   a. live with Officer Sinclair.
   b. ride in Officer Sinclair's police car.
   c. perform service projects as a group.
   d. complete the school courses in self-esteem.

Whole-Story Comprehension

Directions: Read the story below and answer the questions on the following page.

Policeman Next Door

Officer Ellis Sinclair has 33 kids. Sort of. As part of a crime-prevention program, he keeps a close watch on 33 kids, ages 10 to 14. How close? He's moved right into their tough neighborhood!

The police in Macon, Georgia, decided that a group of kids with a history of problems needed their own full-time cop. So the department bought a yellow brick house in East Macon where Sinclair could live and work. He packed everything, even his prized collection of model police cars, and moved in. "The people were glad to see me," he says.

Each week, Officer Sinclair talks to the principal of Appling Middle School to check the students' grades and behavior. He meets with the kids twice a week and listens to them anytime they want to talk. In the summer, the group will go camping, tour a dairy farm, and perform service projects.

The best news: Project Y.E.S. (for Youth Enrichment Services) really seems to work. Before, 88% of the kids in the project had been in trouble with the law. Just 8% have been in trouble since the beginning of the project, and the overall crime rate in East Macon has been lower, too.

A group of neighbors, including Sinclair's own grandmother, helps run Project Y.E.S. They say they feel safer having Sinclair nearby, so they want to help him do his job well. But Sinclair says his work is more than a job. He feels responsible for helping those 33 kids have a better life. Says the officer, who has no kids of his own: "They're my family."

Level 4   **Lesson 15**

Name_____ Date_____

Whole-Story Comprehension *(cont.)*

Directions: After you have read the story on the previous page, answer the questions below.

1. Officer Sinclair moved into
   a. a model police car.
   b. Appling Middle School.
   c. a house bought by the police department.
   d. an apartment building.

2. What is the age range of children involved in the project?
   a. 10–18
   b. 10–14
   c. 8–16
   d. 10–20

3. Y.E.S. is a
   a. program for runaway teens.
   b. program for violent teens.
   c. crime-prevention program.
   d. drug-prevention program.

4. What does Y.E.S. stand for?
   a. Youth Ever Success
   b. Youth Equality Services
   c. Youth Enrichment Services
   d. Youth Environmental Services

5. Who helps run Project Y.E.S.?
   a. a group of neighbors, including Officer Sinclair's grandmother
   b. a group of police officers
   c. parents and teachers
   d. the D.A.R.E. officers

6. The overall crime rate in Macon, Georgia is
   a. increasing.
   b. exhilarating.
   c. decreasing.
   d. staying the same.

7. Before Project Y.E.S., 88% of the kids were in trouble with the law; now only
   a. the boys are in trouble with the law.
   b. 8% of the kids are in trouble with the law.
   c. half of the kids are in trouble with the law.
   d. 2/3 of the kids are in trouble with the law.

8. How does Officer Sinclair feel about the 33 kids?
   a. He is frustrated with their choices.
   b. He is overwhelmed.
   c. He is tired of dealing with them.
   d. He considers them family.

Name_____   Date_____

Enrichment

Directions: Read the information below and use it to answer the following questions.

> In the article, you learned how one man is making a difference in the lives of 33 students. Because of Project Y.E.S. (Youth Enrichment Services), and because of the support and role-modeling of Officer Sinclair, students are learning to make better choices. How does reaching out to troubled youth make a difference with crime prevention?
>
> Getting youth involved not only makes a difference in the life of youth, it also makes a difference in communities. Community service programs designed and led by youth teach specific skills and prevent delinquency by providing opportunities for young people to bond with and improve their communities. The key to success lies in youth participation in designing, selecting, and implementing projects.
>
> Programs like Project Y.E.S. tap into the energy and creativity of young people to make positive changes in their communities. Youth are given the opportunity to carry out projects they've designed to meet their communities' most urgent needs.
>
> Project Y.E.S. also teaches alternatives to violence and delinquency, and teaches a sense of control over one's life, a sense of altruism, and with the help of a consistent presence of a caring adult like Officer Sinclair, builds self-esteem, optimism, and faith in the future. Role models like Officer Sinclair may be some of the only adults youth interact with that are positive individuals.

1. Besides helping the youth, what else is helped by community service projects?

_____

2. What does Project Y.E.S. teach students other than a sense of altruism, self control, and self-esteem?

_____

3. What do role models like Officer Sinclair build for students?

_____

4. What do the letters Y.E.S. stand for?

_____

Level 4   Lesson 15

Name_____   Date_____

Graphic Development

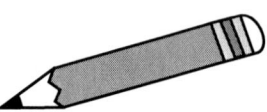

Directions: Read the following information and use the fictional circle graph below to answer the questions below.

> Officer Sinclair has made a big difference in the neighborhood in Macon, Georgia. Crime rates have declined and the number of students in trouble with the law has also declined. Officer Sinclair's dedication to the community is paying off. This summer will bring good things to the neighborhood as well. Students will be filling their time with activities and experiences of a lifetime.
>
> **Super Summer Activities**
>
> (Circle graph with sections: TOURING DAIRY FARMS, CAMPING, SERVICE PROJECTS)

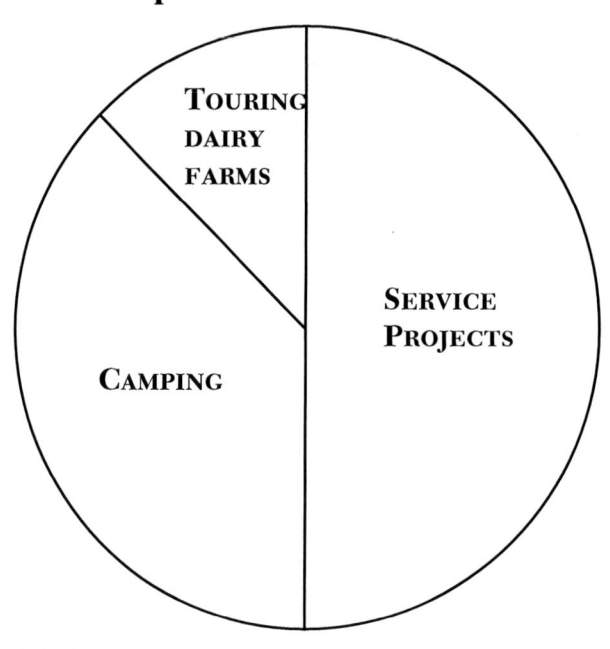

1. What are all the activities that students will be doing this summer?

   _____

2. With which activity will students be spending half of their time?

   _____

3. What is the title of this graph?

   _____

4. Which activity will take the least amount of time?

   _____

5. What activity do you think will be the most popular from the students' perspective?

   _____

#10334 Nonfiction Comprehension Test Practice   ©Shell Educational Publishing

Level 4 Lesson 16

Name_____ Date_____

Sentence Comprehension

Directions: Read the following sentence carefully and answer the questions below "True" (T) or "False" (F).

> Squidzilla is amazing to scientists because it's the most complete and best-preserved giant squid specimen in the world.

1. The scientists think squidzilla is amazing. _____
2. Squidzilla was not very well-preserved. _____
3. Squidzilla is the most complete giant squid specimen. _____
4. Squidzilla is many parts of different squids. _____
5. Squidzilla is still alive. _____

Word Study

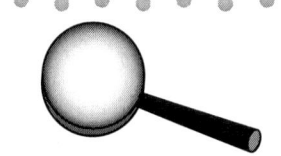

Directions: Read the following information and then change the present tense verbs in the sentences below to past tense verbs.

wrapped

Wrapped means covered by winding or folding. The word wrapped is a verb in the past tense. Past tense verbs are actions that have already been completed or took place at a particular time in the past.

1. _____ I *find* the dog in the garage.
2. _____ We *open* the store at 6:00 A.M. yesterday.
3. _____ Scientists *look* at the squid specimen last week.
4. _____ They never *succeed* in finding another squid.
5. _____ The doctor *complete* the exam by lunchtime.
6. _____ The group *wait* for the news to come out.
7. _____ He wanted the squid specimen *chain* up.
8. _____ No one *wants* the specimen to be ruined.

©Shell Educational Publishing #10334 Nonfiction Comprehension Test Practice

Level 4   Lesson 16

Name_____ Date_____

Paragraph Comprehension

Directions: Read the paragraph below and answer the following questions.

> The squid is in such great shape thanks to quick-thinking fishermen who found it off the coast of New Zealand. When the dead squid landed in one of their giant nets, they froze it right away so the body wouldn't rot. Then it was flown to New York and allowed to defrost overnight at the museum. Next, scientists put it in a bath of special, smelly chemical to preserve it.

1. Which of the following is a true statement?
   a. The squid is in poor shape.
   b. The squid is in good shape because of the scientists.
   c. The squid is in good shape thanks to some quick-thinking fishermen.
   d. The squid is in good shape thanks to squidzilla.

2. Where was the dead squid located?
   a. It was in a fossilized cave.
   b. It landed in a giant net.
   c. It got caught in a rudder.
   d. It was killed in a boat collision.

3. Why did the fishermen freeze the squid?
   a. so it wouldn't rot
   b. because there wasn't enough room in the boat
   c. so it wouldn't fight back
   d. because it was the law

4. The squid was flown to
   a. New Jersey.
   b. New York.
   c. the Smithsonian Museum.
   d. Washington, D.C.

5. What was used to preserve the giant squid specimen?
   a. a base
   b. an acid
   c. a special shampoo
   d. smelly chemicals

ARTICLE FROM TIME FOR KIDS

Name_____ Date_____

Lesson 16

Whole-Story Comprehension

Directions: Read the story below and answer the questions on the following page.

Monster of the Deep

It lies, still and wet, in a huge metal tank wrapped with chains. The case is so big it cannot fit through any of the doors in New York City's American Museum of Natural History. On the side of the case, someone has scratched the letters, "S-Q-U-I-D-Z-I-L-L-A."

"We keep it chained up so it doesn't get out," jokes Neil Landman, a scientist at the museum. There is no way the creature inside that case could get out: it's dead. But what exactly is it?

It's a giant squid, one of the earth's most mysterious animals. No one has ever seen a live giant squid. Scientists have been able to study only a few body parts that have washed up from the ocean over the years.

Squidzilla is amazing to scientists because it's the most complete and best-preserved giant squid specimen in the world. All eight arms are in place!

The squid is in such great shape thanks to quick-thinking fishermen who found it off the coast of New Zealand. When the dead squid landed in one of their giant nets, they froze it right away so the body wouldn't start to rot. Then it was flown to New York and allowed to defrost overnight at the museum. Next, the scientists put it in a bath of special, smelly chemicals to preserve it.

At a length of 25 feet and a weight of 200 pounds, it looked at first to museum scientists like a baby giant squid. Its tentacles are much shorter than those found in the past. Scientists think the biggest giant squid may be as long as 60 feet and weigh more than a ton! But after studying the squid, Landman concluded that it was a full-grown male. "All the other, larger specimens have been female," Landman says. "For the first time, we can infer that there is a difference in size between the males and females."

Giant squids have never been observed in the ocean because they swim in very deep waters—probably as far down as 3,000 feet.

Scientists aren't sure how many of them exist or where in the world the others may live. Don't hold your breath waiting for answers. "Anyone who has gone out to see a giant squid has never succeeded," says Landman. "It is an elusive animal."

©Shell Educational Publishing · #10334 Nonfiction Comprehension Test Practice · 113

Level 4   Lesson 16

Name_____ Date_____

Whole-Story Comprehension *(cont.)*

Directions: After you have read the story on the previous page, answer the questions below.

1. What is Squidzilla?
   a. a monster
   b. a giant squid specimen
   c. a live female squid
   d. a mysterious unknown animal

2. Squidzilla is kept at
   a. the Metropolitan Museum of Arts.
   b. the Smithsonian.
   c. the American Museum of Natural History.
   d. the Oceanic Museum.

3. The amazing part of the squid specimen is
   a. the fact that it is the largest ever found.
   b. that it is still alive.
   c. that the squid was frozen.
   d. that all eight arms are in place.

4. Why have giant squids never been seen?
   a. They are lost.
   b. They are extinct.
   c. They swim in very deep waters.
   d. They are sensitive to the sun.

5. What was the sequence of how the squid was handled?
   a. The squid landed in a net, the fishermen froze the squid, the squid was flown to New York, and then was bathed in special chemicals.
   b. The fishermen froze the squid, the squid was flown to New York, then was bathed in special chemicals, and the squid landed in the net.
   c. The squid landed in a net, the fishermen froze the squid, the squid was bathed in a special chemical, and then the squid was flown to New York.
   d. The squid was immediately flown to New York where it was bathed in special chemicals. Then they discovered the squid in a net.

6. A squid is considered
   a. an elusive animal.
   b. an endangered animal.
   c. food for killer whales.
   d. fish bait.

7. What have scientists inferred about female squids in comparison to male squids?
   a. They are extinct.
   b. They prefer shallow waters.
   c. They are frozen soon after death.
   d. They are larger in size.

8. Which of the following statements is a fact about squids?
   a. Giant squids are beautiful creatures.
   b. A female squid is 20 to 30 feet longer in length than a male squid.
   c. Giant squids look like monsters.
   d. Giant squids need to be chained up.

Level 4   Lesson 16

Name_____ Date_____

Enrichment

Directions: Read the information below and use it to answer the following questions.

What do we know about the giant squid? There really isn't a lot of information because the giant squid is an elusive animal. Read these facts about the giant squid:

- **Where does the giant squid live?**

Few giant squid have ever been seen because they live almost a mile below the surface of the water. Giant squid prefer the deep, cold sea and probably live as far down as 3,000 feet. Warm water causes the squid to rise to the surface and not be able to get down. This is probably why the squid has been so elusive to humans!

- **What does the giant squid eat?**

Giant squid are carnivores, or meat eaters. They eat fish, other squid, and some have even been known to eat whales. The giant squid has a parrot-like beak that is used to rip chunks of flesh from its prey.

- **What is the body of a giant squid like?**

A giant squid is the largest invertebrate. It has a long torpedo-shaped body. A squid has eight arms, or tentacles, and is in the same family as the octopus. Males have been known to be as long as 25 feet and females as long as 60 feet. A squid also has the largest eyes in the animal kingdom. The eyes can be as long as 18 inches across.

- **How long do giant squid live?**

Giant squid have short life cycles, most of them reaching maturity in one to two years. Females grow larger and live longer.

1. What does a giant squid eat?

   _____

2. About how long do male and female squid get?

   _____

3. The giant squid has the largest eyes in the animal kingdom and is also the largest what?

   _____

4. What does the giant squid use to kill its prey?

   _____

5. What does warm water do to the giant squid?

   _____

Level 4   Lesson 16

Name_____   Date_____

Graphic Development

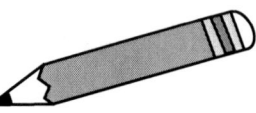

Directions: Use the chart below to answer the questions about large animals of the sea.

Squidzilla has been found! Scientists have determined that female giant squids are longer than male giant squids. The squid in the article was 25 feet long and all eight arms were in place. This is pretty amazing to scientists. Squidzilla is perhaps the largest squid specimen ever found. But is it the largest animal of the sea?

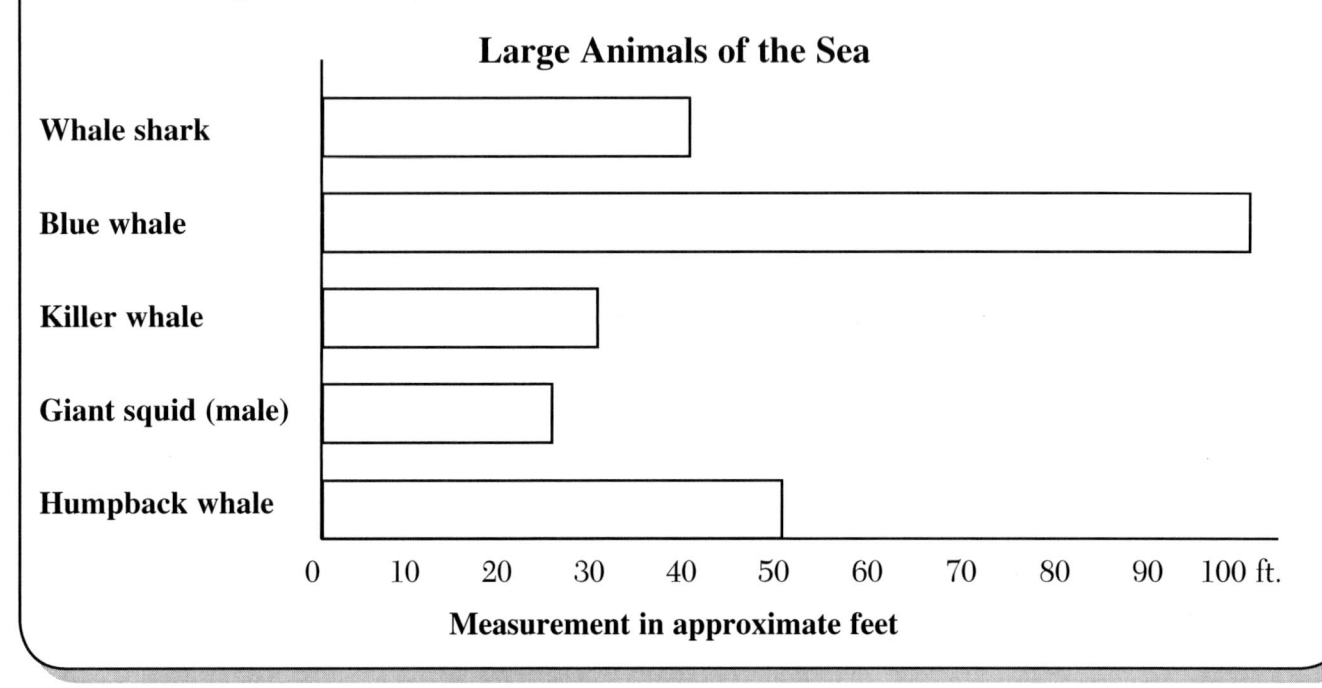

Large Animals of the Sea

Animal	Approximate length (ft)
Whale shark	40
Blue whale	100
Killer whale	30
Giant squid (male)	25
Humpback whale	50

Measurement in approximate feet (0 – 100 ft.)

1. What is the largest animal of the sea?
_____

2. How long is the killer whale?
_____

3. What is the title of the chart?
_____

4. Scientists believe that a female giant squid can get as long as 60 feet. How long does a male giant squid get?
_____

5. What length is the whale shark?
_____

Level 4   **Lesson 17**

Name_____   Date_____

Sentence Comprehension

Directions: Read the following sentence carefully and answer the questions below "True" (T) or "False" (F).

> Computer artists created a golden underwater city, lots of weird-looking aliens, amazing space scenes, and Queen Amidala's wild outfits and hairdos.

1. Computer artists filmed amazing space scenes in outer space. _____
2. The underwater city is made of silver. _____
3. Queen Amidala's outfits and hairdos are boring. _____
4. There are plenty of weird-looking aliens. _____
5. Computer artists created an underwater city. _____

Word Study

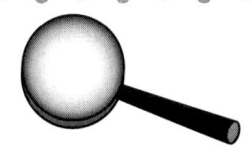

Directions: Read the following information and write the antonym for each of the words below.

antonyms
"good over *evil . . ."* These words are opposites. Words that have opposite meanings are antonyms. Antonyms are useful when clarifying thoughts or making comparisons.

1. _____ cold   7. _____ short
2. _____ dry   8. _____ brave
3. _____ soft   9. _____ good
4. _____ light   10. _____ under
5. _____ strong   11. _____ down
6. _____ day   12. _____ out

©Shell Educational Publishing   #10334 Nonfiction Comprehension Test Practice   117

Level 4   **Lesson 17**

Name_____ Date_____

Paragraph Comprehension

Directions: Read the paragraph below and answer the following questions.

> In 1977, audiences first met Luke Skywalker, Princess Leia, Han Solo, and bad, old Darth Vader. Fans went crazy! They ran to see *Star Wars* again and again. Then they rushed to see what happened next in *The Empire Strikes Back* and *Return of the Jedi*. The films made nearly $2 billion in theaters around the world.

1. What was the response of fans to *Star Wars*?
    a. negative
    b. mediocre
    c. Fans seemed to like it.
    d. Fans went crazy.

2. What was the sequel to *Star Wars*?
    a. *Return of the Jedi*
    b. *The Empire Strikes Back*
    c. *Phantom Menace*
    d. *Star Wars II*

3. How much money did the films make in theaters around the world?
    a. nearly a million dollars
    b. nearly two million dollars
    c. nearly two billion dollars
    d. over 200 million dollars

4. Who were some of the characters in *Star Wars*?
    a. Luke Skywalker and Darth Vader
    b. Queen Amidala and Princess Leia
    c. Jar Jar Binks and Han Solo
    d. Princess Leia and Darth Maul

5. What year did *Star Wars* come out?
    a. 1877
    b. 1977
    c. 1978
    d. 1997

Lesson 17

ARTICLE FROM TIME FOR KIDS

Name_____ Date_____

Whole-Story Comprehension

Directions: Read the story below and answer the questions on the following page.

Feel the Force

In 1977, audiences first met Luke Skywalker, Princess Leia, Han Solo, and bad, old Darth Vader. Fans went crazy! They ran to see *Star Wars* again and again. Then they rushed to see what happened next in *The Empire Strikes Back* and *Return of the Jedi*. The films made nearly $2 billion in theaters around the world.

So the films' creator, George Lucas, decided to take fans back in time before *Star Wars*. *Star Wars: Episode 1—The Phantom Menace* takes place 30 years earlier. Luke and Leia are not born. But we see their mother, the young Queen Amidala, whose kingdom is threatened by the evil warrior, Darth Maul. Their father, Darth Vader, is just an angel-faced kid named Anakin Skywalker. But he shows signs of the Force, the mysterious energy that Jedi knights can control.

The movie is packed with special effects. It has nearly four times as many as *Titanic*. Computer artists created a golden underwater city, lots of weird looking aliens, amazing space scenes, and Queen Amidala's wild outfits and hairdos. The film cost more than $115 million and took four years to complete.

Fans couldn't wait! Some lined up at theaters two months before tickets went on sale. Many had already read the movie's script on the Internet where there were hundreds of Websites about *Phantom Menace*.

Toy stores were ready for the rush, too. Hasbro created 100 action figures, plus other toys, based on the film. Hasbro will make the toys for Episodes II and III also. The company is expected to earn $5 billion from *Star Wars* toys in the next 10 years.

George Lucas makes no apologies for selling *Star Wars* toys. He says the movies' struggles between good and evil are important for kids to think about. He has three kids of his own. He hopes his films will help young people see that choosing good over evil every day makes them heroic. "Heroes come in all sizes," he says. "You can be a very small hero."

The enthusiastic fan reception was repeated again for *Star Wars Episode 2: Attack of the Clones* and *Episode 3: Revenge of the Sith*. These episodes continue the story of Anakin Skywalker's rise as a gifted young Jedi. His eventual fall to the Dark Side of the Force as Darth Vader puts him firmly under the influence of evil Sith Lord Darth Sidious.

Once again, viewers admired the action sequences and special effects in *Episode 2*. Some fans thought that the visual effects were better than those in *The Phantom Menace*. *Revenge of the Sith* is the last of the three films about actions that occurred before the first *Star Wars* movie. It was considered by many fans to be better than *Episodes 1* and *2*.

By any standards, the *Star Wars* series has been a very successful one for George Lucas. The first film released in the series, *Star Wars Episode 4: A New Hope* has been selected to The National Film Registry of the Library of Congress.

Level 4   Lesson 17

Name_____   Date_____

Whole-Story Comprehension *(cont.)*

Directions: After you have read the story on the previous page, answer the questions below.

1. When does *Phantom Menace* take place?
    a. 20 years after *Star Wars*
    b. 30 years before *Star Wars*
    c. 10 years after *Empire Strikes Back*
    d. a sequel to *Star Wars*

2. Who is Anakin Skywalker?
    a. Darth Vader as a boy
    b. Luke Skywalker's son
    c. Jar Jar Binks' hero
    d. Princess Leia's brother

3. The film cost more than $115 million and
    a. went over its budget.
    b. took five years to complete.
    c. took four years to complete.
    d. none of the above

4. *Star Wars* has been selected to the
    a. Motion Picture Academy.
    b. National Education Association.
    c. Good Neighbor Sam Club.
    d. National Film Registry.

5. *Phantom Menace* has four times
    a. the amount of violence than in other movies.
    b. as many special effects as *Titanic*.
    c. as many characters as *Gunsmoke*.
    d. as many sound effects as *Titanic*.

6. The last of the Star Wars films to be made is
    a. *Revenge of the Sith*.
    b. *A New Hope*.
    c. *Attack of the Clones*.
    d. *Return of the Jedi*.

7. Which of the following statements is a fact?
    a. The *Star Wars* movies are cool!
    b. The *Star Wars* movies are liked by everyone.
    c. The *Phantom Menace* is the first of three new *Star Wars* movies.
    d. Darth Vader is the most popular of the characters.

8. Many fans especially liked these features of *Attack of the Clones*:
    a. dialog and color.
    b. plot and dialog.
    c. characters and scenery.
    d. action and special effects.

Enrichment

Directions: Read the information below and use it to answer the following questions.

Have you ever missed a word on a spelling test because you forgot to capitalize it? Capitalization is considered one of the mechanics of writing. The article you just read had many examples of when to use a capital letter. "Feel the Force" capitalized names of people, characters, titles of movies, names of companies, and the beginning words of each sentence. Use the following guidelines to help you remember when to capitalize and when not to capitalize.

Capitalize

- Names of People
- Proper Nouns
- Proper Adjectives
- Historical Events
- Names of a Specific Course
- All Languages, Races, Religions
- Organizations
- Abbreviations
- First Word in a Quotation
- Sections of a Country
- Words/Titles Used as Names
- Titles
- Official Names
- Days of the Week/Month
- First Word in a Sentence

1. Should you capitalize the title of a newspaper?

2. Should you capitalize the sections of a country?

3. What parts of speech should be capitalized?

4. In using quotations, which words in the sentence should be capitalized?

Level 4   Lesson 17

Name_____   Date_____

Graphic Development

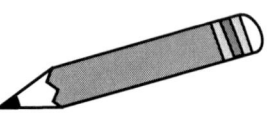

Directions: Read the following information and use the Venn diagram to answer the questions below.

Star Wars movies have made their mark! The enthusiasm for weird aliens and the mysterious energy that only Jedi knights can control has made a comeback. One of the movies is *Episode I—The Phantom Menace*. Just what are the similarities and differences between this flick and the original?

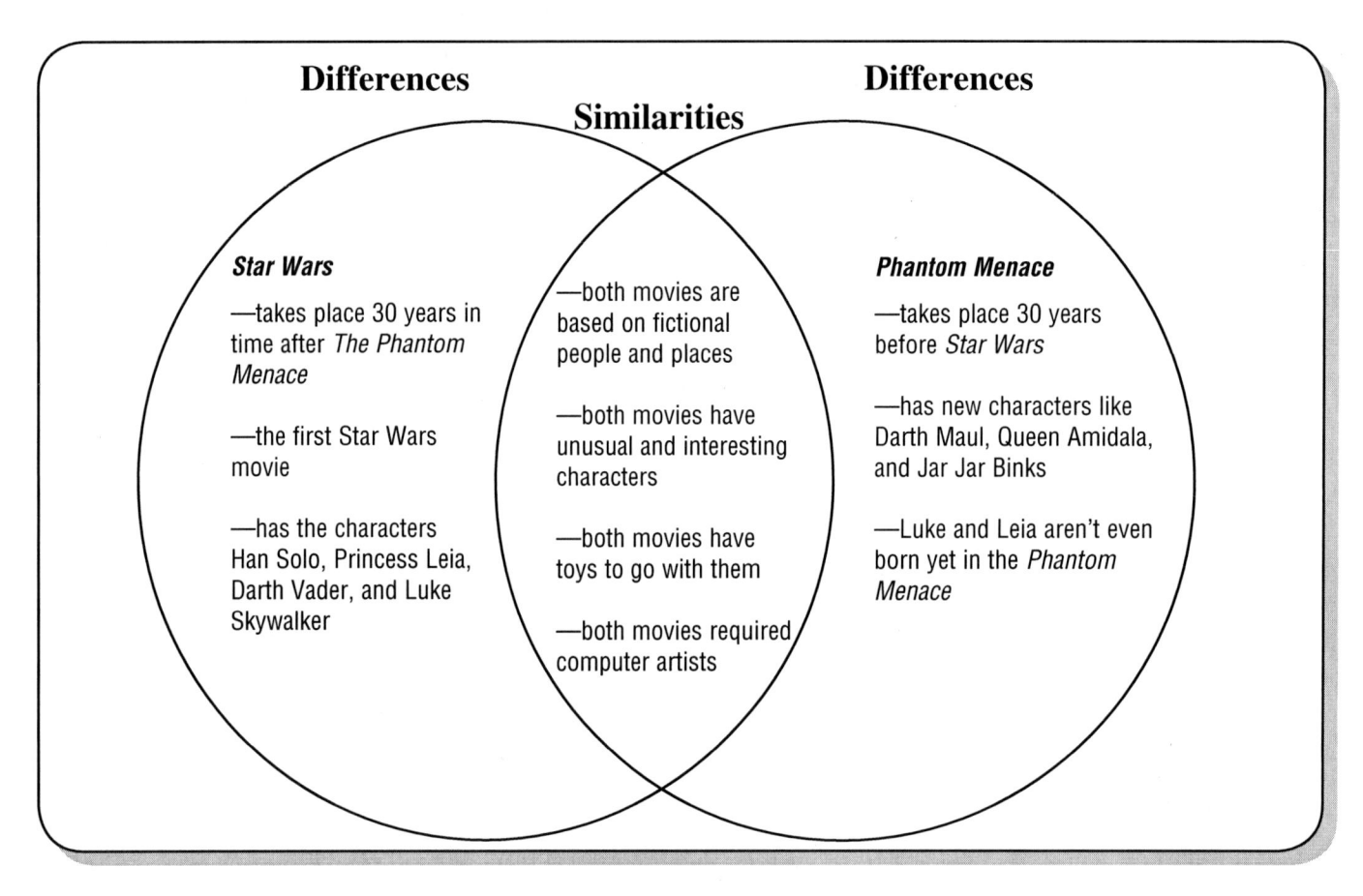

Differences   **Differences**
                   Similarities

Star Wars
—takes place 30 years in time after *The Phantom Menace*

—the first Star Wars movie

—has the characters Han Solo, Princess Leia, Darth Vader, and Luke Skywalker

—both movies are based on fictional people and places

—both movies have unusual and interesting characters

—both movies have toys to go with them

—both movies required computer artists

Phantom Menace
—takes place 30 years before *Star Wars*

—has new characters like Darth Maul, Queen Amidala, and Jar Jar Binks

—Luke and Leia aren't even born yet in the *Phantom Menace*

1. What information can be gathered from this Venn diagram?
   _____

2. What are two of the similarities between the two movies?
   _____

3. Which movie has the character of Queen Amidala?
   _____

4. Both movies require what type of artist to be used?
   _____

5. Which movie has toys to go with the movie characters?
   _____

Level 4   Lesson 18

Name_____ Date_____

Sentence Comprehension

Directions: Read the following sentence carefully and answer the questions below "True" (T) or "False" (F).

> Kids also love to laugh, and *Goosebumps* episodes make kids laugh through a thrill of fear.

1. Episodes of *Goosebumps* are for adults only. _____
2. Kids love to laugh. _____
3. *Goosebumps* episodes just scare kids. _____
4. *Goosebumps* is a new video game. _____
5. *Goosebumps* episodes are meant to scare and entertain. _____

Word Study

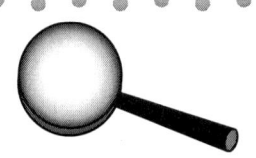

Directions: Read the following information and write an adjective from the list to describe the noun in each sentence below.

> **vicious**
>
> In the article, the beast was described as vicious. Vicious means dangerously aggressive. Beast is a noun and vicious is an adjective. An adjective is a word that describes the noun.

enormous   wicked   fun   cute   small   new

1. The _____ beast could barely fit through the door.
2. There is only a _____ piece of pie left.
3. The kids that read the books say they are _____ books to read.
4. The _____ nightmare wasn't the same as the others.
5. All of the kids ran after the _____ little puppy.
6. Eddie and Sue met up with a _____ witch in the story as well.

©Shell Educational Publishing   #10334 Nonfiction Comprehension Test Practice

| Level 4 | Lesson 18 |

Name_____ Date_____

Paragraph Comprehension

Directions: Read the paragraph below and answer the following questions.

> Not convinced? Just listen! Imagine going with Sue and Eddie for a "Night in Terror Tower." As their parents attend a meeting at the hotel, these 13- and 11-year-olds tour London. The kids look forward to the tour bus stop at Terror Tower. This tower was a prison and torture chamber during the Middle Ages.

1. "Night in Terror Tower" is probably

   a. the name of a store.
   b. the title of a book.
   c. a nightmare.
   d. the sequel to a movie.

2. How old are Eddie and Sue?

   a. 6 and 8
   b. 9 and 11
   c. 11 and 13
   d. 14 and 16

3. Sue and Eddie are looking forward to

   a. getting home.
   b. touring Terror Tower.
   c. going on vacation.
   d. school starting up again.

4. Where are their parents?

   a. they stayed home
   b. they are lost in Terror Tower
   c. attending a meeting in the hotel
   d. lost

5. What was Terror Tower?

   a. the name of a book
   b. the tallest part of a haunted house
   c. part of Eddie and Sue's dream
   d. a torture chamber during the Middle Ages

Whole-Story Comprehension

Directions: Read the story below and answer the questions on the following page.

Goosebumps TV

If you are like most kids, you like to read *Goosebumps* and you love TV. If this describes you, you won't want to miss watching the TV videos and DVDs of R.L. Stine's *Goosebumps* stories.

Stine is the Pied Piper of children. His books have attracted millions of young readers. In fact, R.L. Stine titles sell over a million copies a month! The magic carries over to video and DVD. What is it about these stories that makes them irresistible?

Kids love to be scared and Stine's tales are scary. Kids also love to laugh, and *Goosebumps* episodes make kids laugh through a thrill of fear. They are filled with turns, surprises, and funny jokes. Unlike most videos and DVDs, *Goosebumps* endings are unpredictable.

The combination of mystery, horror, and adventure is enough to grab any kid's interest. And your parents can relax. The episodes are designed to give shivers, not nightmares. The scares are mild-mannered.

Not convinced? Just listen! Imagine going with Sue and Eddie for a "Night in Terror Tower." As their parents attend a meeting at the hotel, these 13- and 11-year olds tour London. The kids look forward to the tour bus stop at Terror Tower. This tower was a prison and torture chamber during the Middle Ages.

At the tower, however, strange things begin to happen that only Eddie and Sue can see. The figures begin to move as if real. The only children on the tour are also the only ones to hear the ghostly warnings. Then the guide tells a tale about a prince and princess sentenced to die in the tower five hundred years ago. Without warning, the children find themselves separated from the group. Stranger and more haunting things happen to Sue and Eddie as they are drawn toward the fate meant for the prince and princess.

Is that too fantastic for you? "Welcome to Camp Nightmare" brings viewers into a scene that is familiar to many kids. At first, Camp Nightmare seems like the summer camp of Billy's dreams. It has basketball, archery, and a big lake. Then really weird stuff starts happening. Billy is worried about a mysterious, vicious beast called Sabre. Fellow campers start disappearing, one by one. Mike is bitten by a snake. Roger is attacked by a creature in the woods. Then, Jay and Colin disappear in the lake. Afraid he is next, Billy is determined to find out what is going on.

These episodes, and many others, offer kids, eight and older, a hair-raisingly fun getaway. Kids are tuning in. So should you. Stine spins just as good a tale on video as on paper.

Level 4 Lesson 18

Name_____ Date_____

Whole-Story Comprehension (cont.)

Directions: After you have read the story on the previous page, answer the questions below.

1. Who is R.L. Stine?
   a. the author of *Goosebumps* books
   b. a character in *Goosebumps* books
   c. the father of Eddie and Sue
   d. the TV producer of *Goosebumps*

2. What group are *Goosebumps* books geared to?
   a. small children
   b. high school children
   c. kids eight and older
   d. mostly boys

3. What do kids like about the books?
   a. They have hard covers.
   b. They have free decoder rings.
   c. They are horror stories.
   d. They are a combination of mystery, horror, and adventure.

4. What happens in the "Tower of Terror"?
   a. The children hear screaming.
   b. Wax figures begin to move as though they are real.
   c. Sue and Eddie can't find their parents.
   d. Sue and Eddie find the prince and princess.

5. What happens to Billy's fellow campers at Camp Nightmare?
   a. They steal the food.
   b. They begin to disappear.
   c. They flood the tent.
   d. They get lost in the woods.

6. What makes *Goosebumps* episodes different than other TV programs?
   a. The endings are unpredictable.
   b. The endings are all the same.
   c. There are no commercials.
   d. The endings are incomplete.

7. The author, R.L. Stine,
   a. sells bookmarks to go with his books.
   b. bases his stories on real-life adventures.
   c. sells over a million copies in a month.
   d. writes a sequel to each story he writes.

8. The author of this article
   a. likes the books by R.L. Stine.
   b. thinks the *Goosebumps* books are silly.
   c. is discouraging people from reading *Goosebumps*.
   d. is warning parents of the content in R.L. Stine books.

Enrichment

Directions: Read the information below and use it to answer the following questions.

> The title, *Goosebumps TV,* is actually an abbreviation! The word TV is the shortened form of the word television. Other examples of abbreviated words are CD (compact disc) and DVD (digital video disk).
>
> Zipf's principle is the term used for this. Zipf's principle is the shortening of words from common use, as in *ad* for *advertisement*. Words that have been shortened are now called abbreviations or clipped words. Clipped words often become more frequently used than the original words. Look at the examples below.
>
> ad = advertisement   fridge = refrigerator
> burger = hamburger   gym = gymnasium
> photo = photograph   tux = tuxedo
> fan = fanatic   taxi = taxicab
> sub = submarine

Now look at the clipped words below. What was the original word? Write it in the space. The first one has been done for you.

1. memo   *memorandum*
2. grad   _____
3. champ   _____
4. bike   _____
5. vet   _____
6. trig   _____
7. auto   _____
8. math   _____
9. phone   _____
10. con   _____

Level 4   Lesson 18

Name_____   Date_____

Graphic Development

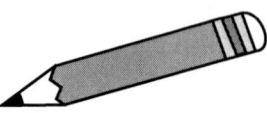

Directions: Read the following information and use the bar graph of Mr. Minket's fifth grade class to answer the questions below.

> *Goosebumps* stories by R.L. Stine are guaranteed to cause a chill. Stine is able to weave a scary story with surprises and funny jokes. Children eight years and older love to be scared. With the new TV episodes expected out soon, just which of the *Goosebumps* stories should become episodes?
>
> **R.L. Stine Favorites**
>
> (Bar graph — Number of Students vs. R.L. Stine Books:
> Full Moon Fever: 6; Night in Terror Tower: 8; Welcome to Camp Nightmare: 7)

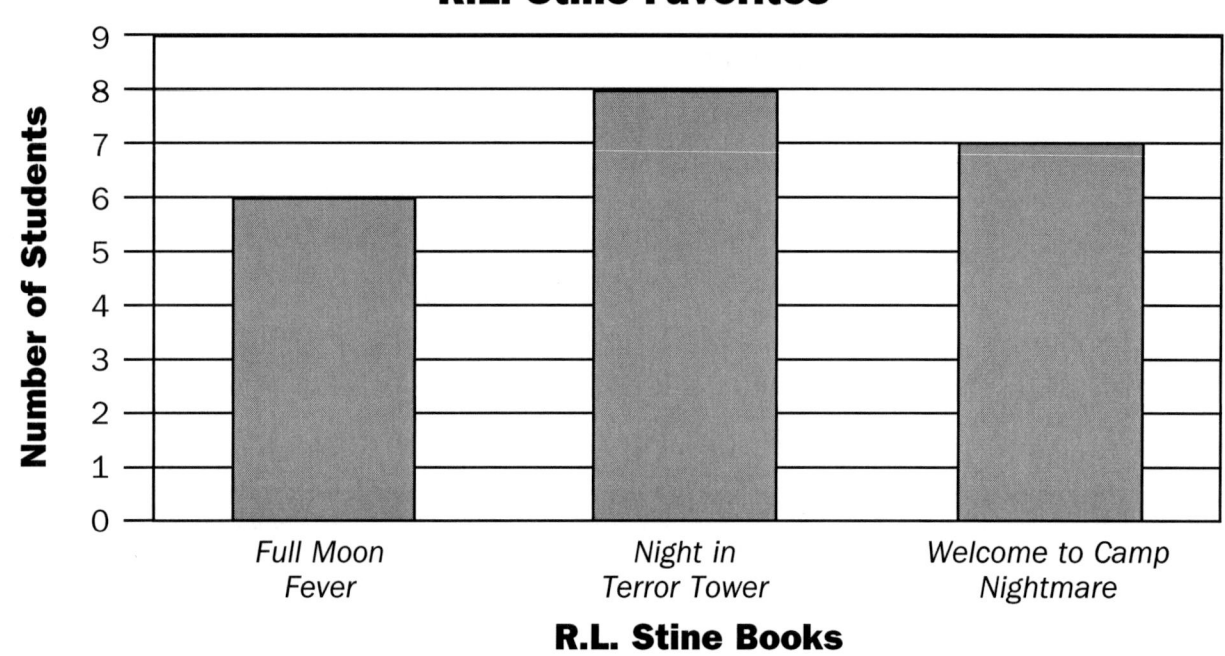

1. Which book did most of the students pick as their favorite R.L. Stine book?
   _____

2. What is the total number of students that are in Mr. Minket's class?
   _____

3. From many of R.L. Stine's books did students have to pick?
   _____

4. How many more students like *Night in Terror Tower* more than *Full Moon Fever*?
   _____

5. Does this graph show the differences of opinion between male and female students?
   _____

Level 4 Lesson 19

Name_____ Date_____

Sentence Comprehension

Directions: Read the following sentence carefully and answer the questions below "True" (T) or "False" (F).

> However, Harry's family is more like the wicked stepmother and stepsisters of *Cinderella* than the strict parents of realistic stories.

1. Harry lives with a wicked stepmother and stepsisters. _____
2. Harry's family is similar to Cinderella's family. _____
3. Harry's story is a sequel to *Cinderella*. _____
4. Harry enjoys living with his family. _____
5. Harry's family is probably more strict than most strict parents. _____

Word Study

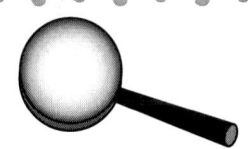

Directions: Read the following information and write the prefix of the words on the lines before each word.

unusual

Unusual means uncommon, not usual, or rare. *Unusual* begins with the common prefix, /un/. A prefix comes before the root word. Prefixes can often change the meaning of words.

1. _____ hyperactive
2. _____ interrupt
3. _____ circumstance
4. _____ catalogue
5. _____ copilot

6. _____ semicircle
7. _____ hexagon
8. _____ introduce
9. _____ intervene
10. _____ extraordinary

©Shell Educational Publishing   #10334 Nonfiction Comprehension Test Practice   **129**

Level 4   Lesson 19

Name_____   Date_____

Paragraph Comprehension

Directions: Read the paragraph below and answer the following questions.

> Harry finally escapes from his awful aunt and uncle. He is sent by friends of his parents to a school called Hogwarts. Hogwarts has unusual classes involving magic. However, it also includes strict rules and competition among students that real kids experience. The most popular game at Hogwarts is Quidditch, a kind of hockey played on flying broomsticks.

1. Harry is able to escape

   a. Hogwarts.
   b. his aunt and uncle.
   c. his parents and friends.
   d. Quidditch.

2. Where was Harry sent?

   a. to Hogwarts, a school
   b. to the orphanage
   c. back to his aunt and uncle's house
   d. to live with his grandfather

3. What are the classes like at Hogwarts?

   a. They are full of spoiled boys.
   b. They are taught in a foreign language.
   c. They involve magic.
   d. They are difficult to pass.

4. Quidditch is

   a. a tough course at Hogwarts.
   b. the name of the school Harry attends.
   c. Harry's last name.
   d. a game like hockey played on broomsticks.

5. How is Hogwarts similar to school that real kids experience?

   a. It has teachers.
   b. It has competition among the students.
   c. It has extracurricular activities.
   d. It has a principal.

130   #10334 Nonfiction Comprehension Test Practice   ©Shell Educational Publishing

Whole-Story Comprehension

Directions: Read the story below and answer the questions on the following page.

A Review of Harry Potter and the Sorcerer's Stone

Some books are fun because they are true to life. You can easily identify with the characters. Other books take kids to an imaginary universe. From fairy tales like *Alice in Wonderland* to the *Chronicles of Narnia*, they create a new world that's similar to our own, but with magical differences. A great new series of books about a boy named Harry Potter creates a fantasy world that kids will love to visit.

J.K. Rowling's first book about Harry is called *Harry Potter and the Sorcerer's Stone*. Harry lives in a place that seems in some ways like modern-day Great Britain. Harry has problems like real kids. His parents died when he was a baby. He doesn't get along with the aunt and uncle with whom he lives. His cousin is a spoiled brat and a bully. However, Harry's family is more like the wicked stepmother and stepsisters of *Cinderella* than the strict parents of realistic stories. For example, Harry's aunt and uncle give their son Dudley two bedrooms: one to sleep in and one in which to keep his extra toys. Harry has no toys and must sleep in a cupboard.

Harry, though, has magical powers. He also has some very unusual adults on his side. For example, Hagrid is a giant twice as tall as normal men. When Harry's aunt and uncle keep Harry from getting important mail about his future, Hagrid steps in.

Harry finally escapes from his awful aunt and uncle. He is sent by friends of his parents to a school called Hogwarts. Hogwarts has unusual classes involving magic. However, it also includes strict rules and competition among students that real kids experience. The most popular game at Hogwarts is Quidditch, a kind of hockey played on flying broomsticks.

Kids will root for Harry, who is brave and smart, but not perfect. Will Harry find the Sorcerer's Stone? Will his team win at Quidditch? Most importantly, will the headmaster, Albus Dumbledore, tell Harry what really happened to his parents? Kids will love the fantasy world in this book.

If you read and like *Sorcerer's Stone*, you may want to read the rest of the series: *Harry Potter and the Chamber of Secrets, the Prisoner of Azkaban, the Goblet of Fire, the Order of the Phoenix, the Half-Blood Prince*—and what Rowling calls "HP7."

Rowling wrote on her Website that she never planned to write any more novels "after HP7." She explained that she had "enough story for seven books" and "never planned to carry the story beyond the end of book seven." If she does write anything, she added, it might be an eighth book for charity, but not a novel.

Whole-Story Comprehension (cont.)

Directions: After you have read the story on the previous page, answer the questions below.

1. Harry Potter books are
   a. comic books.
   b. romance novels.
   c. fiction books.
   d. fantasy books.

2. This article is
   a. encouraging young kids to try magic.
   b. endorsing strict rules in public schools.
   c. a review of the book, *Harry Potter and the Sorcerer's Stone*.
   d. negative about Harry Potter books.

3. Who is J.K. Rowling?
   a. author of Harry Potter books
   b. publisher of Harry Potter books
   c. mother of Harry Potter
   d. fan of Harry Potter books

4. Harry lives in a place similar to
   a. a town you live in.
   b. a fantasy world.
   c. modern-day Great Britain.
   d. New York City.

5. Where does Harry sleep at his aunt's house?
   a. in the upstairs bedroom
   b. at the Quidditch
   c. in a cupboard
   d. with his cousin, Dudley

6. Harry is considered
   a. shy and quiet.
   b. brave and smart.
   c. brave, yet foolish.
   d. angry and frustrated.

7. Hagrid is
   a. Harry's roommate at Hogwart's.
   b. an enemy Harry is afraid of.
   c. a giant twice as tall as normal men.
   d. a giant out to get Harry's parents.

8. Who is Albus Dumbledore?
   a. Harry's father
   b. a wizard
   c. the sorcerer
   d. the Headmaster at Hogwarts

Level 4 — Lesson 19

Name_____   Date_____

Enrichment

Directions: Read the information below and use it to answer the following questions.

> Read these sentences taken from the article that you just read. Note the use of commas in these sentences.
>
> *However, Harry's family is more like the wicked stepmother and stepsisters of "Cinderella" than the strict parents of realistic stories.*
>
> *Harry, though, has magical powers.*
>
> *When Harry's aunt and uncle keep Harry from getting important mail about the future, Hagrid steps in.*
>
> *Most importantly, will the headmaster, Albus Dumbledore, tell Harry what really happened to his parents?*
>
> How do you know when to use a comma? A comma is used in a series of words, to set off dialogue, and between two clauses. Look at the following examples:
>
> **Series of Words**
> I will bring the milk, cookies, and bread.
>
> **To set off Dialogue**
> The mother sat up and said, "I think I can handle that."
>
> **Between Two Clauses**
> After I read the note, I turned pale.

Write the reasons why commas have been used in these sentences.

1. Harry Potter was wondering what he was to do with the baking soda, clay, and food coloring.

_____

2. The game of Quidditch was taking longer than planned and Professor Dumbledore shouted, "Time's up!"

_____

3. After she woke up, Sally brushed her teeth.

_____

Level 4   Lesson 19

Name_____ Date_____

Graphic Development

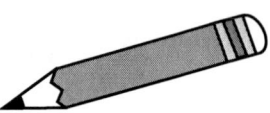

Directions: Read the following information and use the character web to analyze the characters from Harry Potter.

J.K. Rowling has created a wonderful world of fantasy in her series about Harry Potter. The characters and plots are complex and intriguing. Which characters are out to get Harry and which ones will offer support?

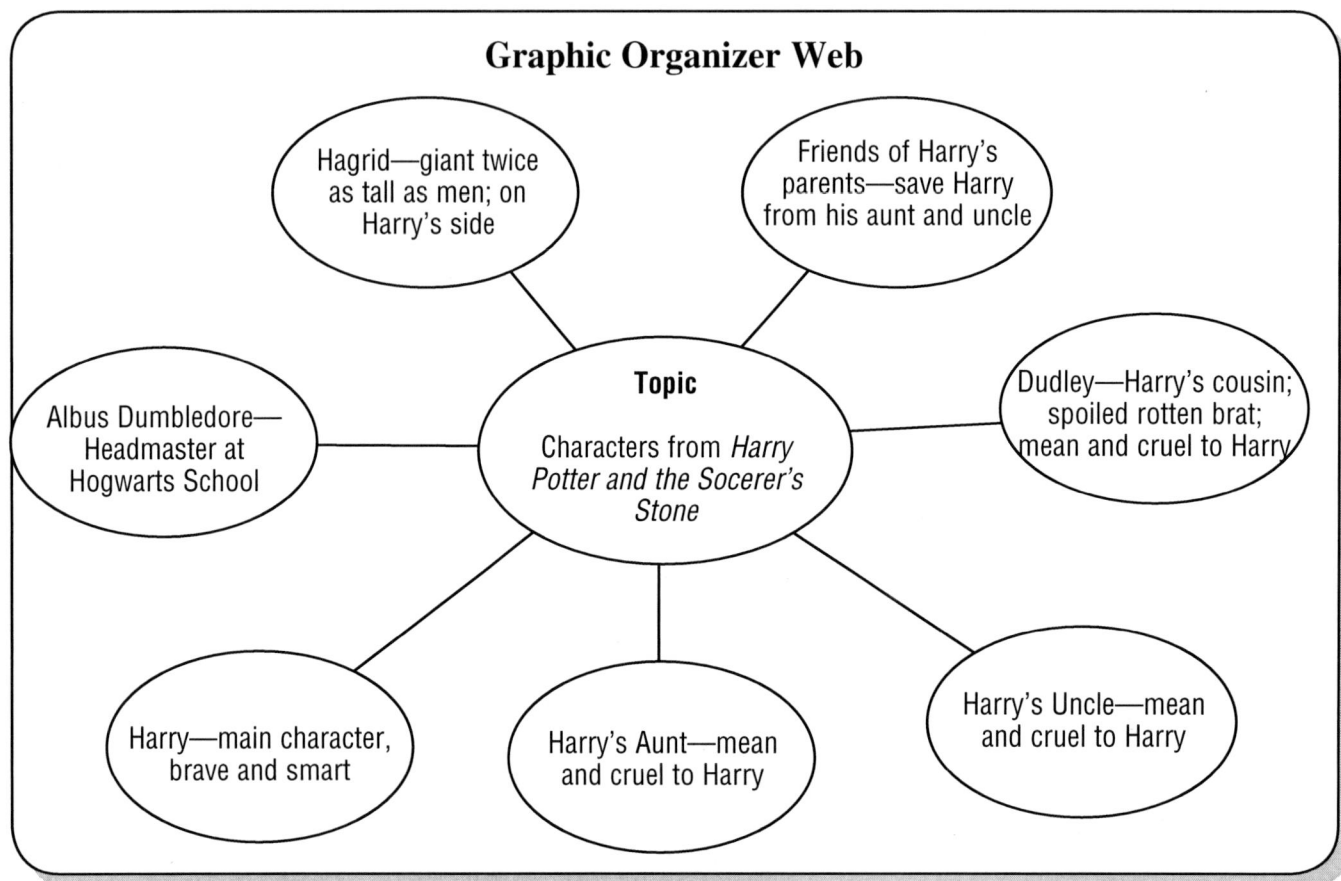

Graphic Organizer Web

- Hagrid—giant twice as tall as men; on Harry's side
- Friends of Harry's parents—save Harry from his aunt and uncle
- Albus Dumbledore—Headmaster at Hogwarts School
- Dudley—Harry's cousin; spoiled rotten brat; mean and cruel to Harry
- **Topic:** Characters from *Harry Potter and the Socerer's Stone*
- Harry—main character, brave and smart
- Harry's Aunt—mean and cruel to Harry
- Harry's Uncle—mean and cruel to Harry

1. What is the topic of the character web?

   _____

2. Who is Harry's headmaster at Hogwarts?

   _____

3. How many of the characters seem to be against Harry?

   _____

4. Name two things about the character Hagrid.

   _____

5. Who is the main character in *Harry Potter and the Sorcerer's Stone?*

   _____

Level 4 **Lesson 20**

Name_____ Date_____

Sentence Comprehension

Directions: Read the following sentence carefully and answer the questions below "True" (T) or "False" (F).

> The whales you see in zoos, aquariums, and ocean theme parks are living confined, uncomfortable lives.

1. Whales are uncomfortable living outside of their natural environment. _____
2. Whales are kept in zoos, aquariums, and ocean theme parks. _____
3. Whales are confined if they live in zoos, but not ocean theme parks. _____
4. Aquariums are the best habitats for the whales. _____
5. This sentence is about how a whale is born. _____

Word Study

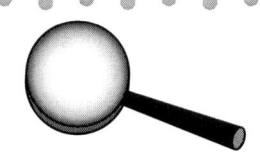

Directions: Read the following information in the box. On the lines below, write only units of measurement that indicate length.

> **mile**
>
> A mile is a unit of measurement. There are many different words used to express measurement. Length, weight, capacity, volume, square measure, and land measure are all categories of measurement words. Mile is a measurement of length.

inches	yards	quarts	feet	kiloliters
miles	milliliters	tons	gallons	
centimeters	grams	pounds	decimeters	
	liters		cups	

1. _____   4. _____

2. _____   5. _____

3. _____   6. _____

Level 4   Lesson 20

Name_____ Date_____

Paragraph Comprehension

Directions: Read the paragraph below and answer the following questions.

> While Keiko was getting stronger, his caretakers were busy designing a new home for him in Iceland. Because Keiko had lived almost his whole life in captivity, it was too risky to just set him free. The solution was to build a giant floating pen in the North Atlantic Ocean. The pen is 250 feet long and has walls made of special nets so that fish can swim in and out. Keiko can see and hear nearby whales and birds.

1. Where was a home built for Keiko?

    a. Iceland
    b. Greenland
    c. Arctic
    d. Sea World

2. Why couldn't they just set Keiko free?

    a. They couldn't find him.
    b. He was unable to feed himself.
    c. He had lived his whole life in captivity.
    d. He was under contract with the movie producers.

3. In which ocean was the pen for Keiko built?

    a. Indian Ocean
    b. North Atlantic Ocean
    c. Arctic Ocean
    d. Pacific Ocean

4. What type of pen was built for Keiko?

    a. a glass pen so Keiko could see outside
    b. a floating pen with special nets
    c. an aquarium with heated water
    d. a large pen to fit Keiko's family

5. What can Keiko hear and see from his pen?

    a. short, high sounds
    b. whales in nearby cages
    c. nearby whales and birds
    d. his movie fans

Lesson 20

ARTICLE FROM TIME FOR KIDS

Name_____ Date_____

Whole-Story Comprehension

Directions: Read the story below and answer the questions on the following page.

Captivity Equals Cruelty for Whales

Most killer whales swim thousands of miles in their lifetimes. They travel long distances while hunting seals, sea lions, and dolphins. But some whales are captured and live in small pools to be observed by people. The whales you see at zoos, aquariums, and ocean theme parks are living confined, uncomfortable lives.

One whale that has lived an unnatural life of captivity is Keiko. He was the killer whale that starred in the 1993 movie *Free Willy*.

Keiko's journey began in the frosty blue waters of the Atlantic Ocean near Iceland, where he was born about 20 years ago. At age two, he was captured and taken to an aquarium in Iceland. He would never swim with his pod (family group) again.

Soon after that, he was moved to an aquarium in Canada, and began performing tricks for people. But he didn't make his big splash until an aquarium in Mexico bought him. That's where he landed the lead whale role in *Free Willy*. The hit movie made Keiko a Hollywood heavyweight.

In the movie, Keiko's character suffers through awful living conditions in a theme park. In real life, Keiko's situation wasn't any better. His pool at the aquarium in Mexico was too small and too warm. His skin, once glossy and slick, broke out in sores. Also, the big fin on his back, called a dorsal fin, flopped sadly over to one side.

Keiko's fans rushed to his rescue. A group called the Free Willy Foundation raised enough money to fly him from Mexico to a specially built pool in Newport, Oregon, in 1996. In his new cool pool (just 45 degrees Fahrenheit), Keiko's health improved right away. His skin sores disappeared and he gained 2,000 pounds. Soon he was strong enough for a journey home.

While Keiko was getting stronger, his caretakers were busy designing a new home for him in Iceland. Because Keiko had lived almost his whole life in captivity, it was too risky just to set him free. The solution was to build a giant floating pen in the North Atlantic Ocean. The pen was 250 feet long and had walls made of special nets so that fish swam in and out. Keiko could see and hear nearby whales.

Although some people thought Keiko's move was stressful, he was still far more fortunate than other whales that have been captured. It is impossible to create a healthy environment for a whale in an aquarium or other home created by people. Suppose the temperature and chemical makeup of the water are carefully controlled. A pool is still too tiny to serve as the home of an animal that may way up to 10 tons. In addition, a captive animal cannot be near its natural neighbors —fish, birds, and other ocean animals. It certainly cannot travel the world's oceans.

Whales are fun to observe. But the next time you see a whale in an aquarium or theme park, ask yourself this question: Is it okay to pen up a beautiful animal in an unnatural, possibly unhealthy environment so that people can look at it? Whales are among the world's most fascinating animals. Let's allow them to live peacefully in the ocean. In 2003, Keiko died of pneumonia in the Taknes fjord, Norway.

Level 4   Lesson 20

Name_____   Date_____

Whole-Story Comprehension (cont.)

Directions: After you have read the story on the previous page, answer the questions below.

1. How is the life of a free killer whale different than one in captivity?
    a. They are larger whales.
    b. They are trained by trainers.
    c. They can swim thousands of miles.
    d. They are paid lots of money.

2. At what age was Keiko captured?
    a. five
    b. two
    c. four
    d. ten

3. What were the conditions like in Mexico for Keiko?
    a. frigid water
    b. too small and too warm
    c. too large and spacious
    d. small enough but water was too warm

4. Who helped Keiko?
    a. his trainer
    b. his doctor
    c. his fans with the Free Willy Foundation
    d. his movie crew

5. Where was Keiko sent to recover?
    a. Iceland
    b. Mexico
    c. Canada
    d. Newport, Oregon

6. Keiko is a
    a. whale.
    b. movie producer.
    c. famous actress.
    d. consumer.

7. Even with temperatures and climate controls,
    a. the pool was still not the best option.
    b. Keiko was able to escape.
    c. Keiko began to grow.
    d. Keiko was released.

8. How heavy can a whale get?
    a. over 500 pounds
    b. up to 10 tons
    c. over 16 tons
    d. over 30,000 tons

Name_____ Date_____

Enrichment

Directions: Read the information below and use it to answer the following questions.

There are two different groups of whales. There are the baleen whales and the toothed whales. Baleen whales have baleen which are used to sieve food from the seawater. These types of whales are considered filter feeders. Here are three types of baleen whales.

Blue Whale—A blue whale is the largest animal and the largest whale. A blue whale is pale blue-gray in color and has a long streamlined body. Blue whales are often found alone or in pairs. There are approximately 6,000 to 14,000 blue whales, and they are on the endangered species list. Blue whales eat krill or other crustaceans.

Humpback Whale—Humpback whales can dive for three to nine minutes and have a pronounced hump in front of their fin on top. There are approximately 12,000–15,000 humpback whales. Humpback whales can weigh 25–30 tons and eat krill and other crustaceans.

Minke Whale—The population of minke whales is approximately 500,000 to one million. Minke whales gather into groups of one on up to 100 at good feeding sites. Minke whales are a pale-gray/bluish-gray color with white on the under side. Minke whales have been seen swimming alongside a boat.

Toothed whales have teeth and eat their food with teeth instead of with baleen. Here are two toothed whales.

Killer Whale—Keiko, from the article, is a killer whale. Another name for a killer whale is an orca. Killer whales eat fish, and occasionally squid and octopus. Killer whales live in pods of groups from three to 25. Killer whales have teeth which curve back toward the throat. Killer whales can travel up to 34 mph.

Bottlenose Dolphin—Bottlenose dolphins are whales and are powerful swimmers and divers. They live in groups ranging from one to hundreds in the ocean. Bottlenose dolphins have teeth and eat fish, squid, krill, and other crustaceans.

---

1. Which of the whales described above are baleen whales? _____

2. What is the difference between baleen whales and toothed whales? _____

3. How fast can a killer whale swim? _____

4. Which of the above whales is on the endangered species list? _____

5. Which whale has a hump in front of its fin? _____

Level 4   Lesson 20

Name_____ Date_____

Graphic Development

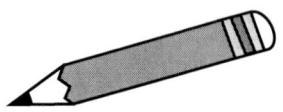

Directions: Read the following information and use the map below to answer the questions.

Keiko the whale is probably the most popular whale ever known, but he has paid a price for his popularity. Keiko has lived most of his life in captivity. Keiko was captured in the Atlantic Ocean near Iceland. He was taken to an aquarium in Iceland. From there he was moved to Canada, Mexico, Oregon, and back to Iceland. Keiko spent most of his time in and around the oceans of the North American continent.

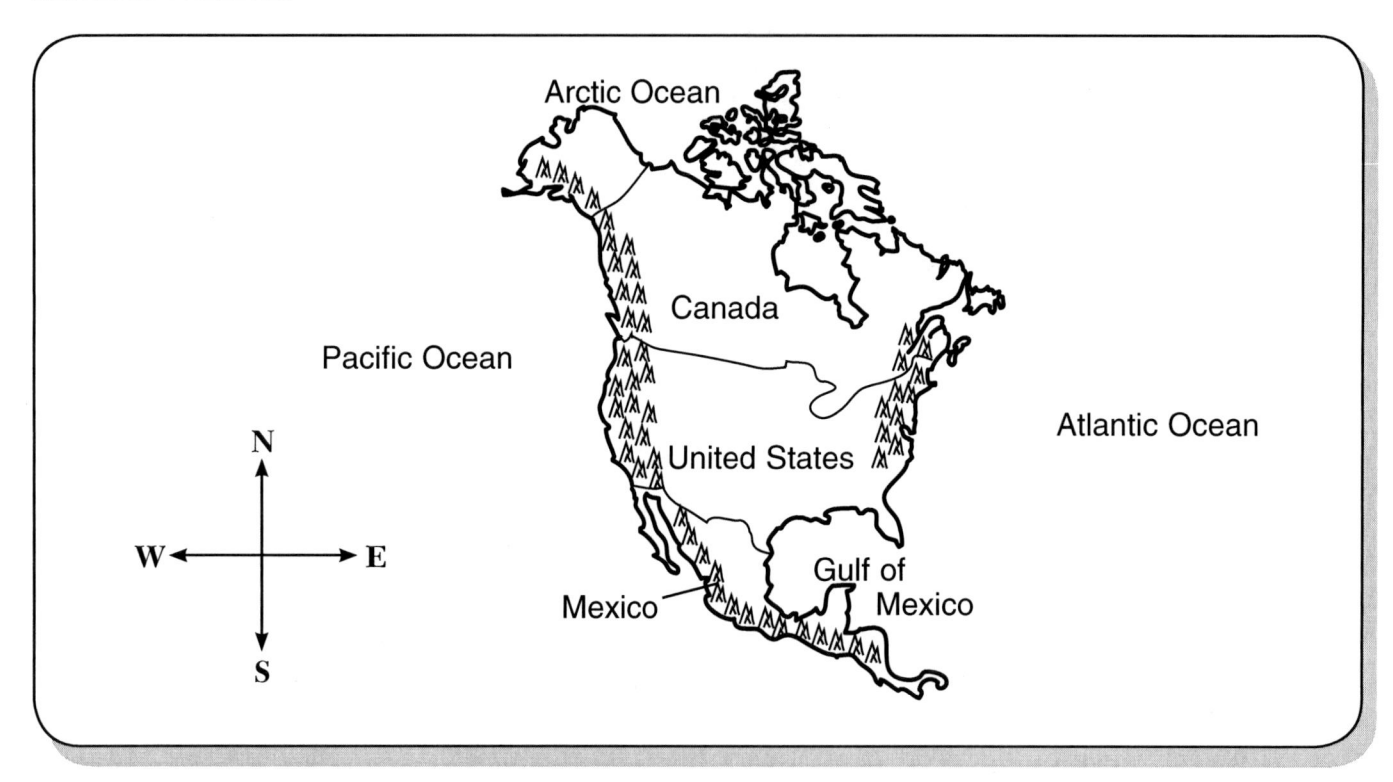

1. Most of the mountains are in what part of the North American continent?
   _____

2. What is the name of the ocean where Keiko was captured? Is it east or west of North America?
   _____

3. Newport, Oregon, is on the northwest corner of the United States. What ocean is near there?
   _____

4. Keiko spent some of his time in Mexico. Is Mexico north or south of the U.S.?
   _____

5. What ocean is at the northernmost part of the North American continent?
   _____

140   #10334 Nonfiction Comprehension Test Practice   ©Shell Educational Publishing

Answer Key

Lesson 1
Page 21
Sentence Comprehension
1. F
2. F
3. F
4. T
5. T

Word Study
1. all-purpose
2. X-ray
3. dot-matix
4. T-bone
5. PG-rated
6. Fourteen-year-old

Page 22
Paragraph Comprehension
1. a
2. c
3. d
4. b
5. b

Page 24
Whole-Story Comprehension
1. b
2. c
3. c
4. c
5. a
6. a
7. d
8. a

Page 25
Enrichment
1. G
2. B
3. C
4. E
5. D
6. A
7. F

Page 26
Graphic Development
1. Arm Control
2. Reading or Sight
3. Face Control
4. Sight
5. Speech
6. Hearing
7. Leg Control

Lesson 2
Page 27
Sentence Comprehension
1. F
2. F
3. T
4. F
5. F

Word Study
Answers will vary.

Page 28
Paragraph Comprehension
1. b
2. c
3. d
4. d
5. c

Page 30
Whole-Story Comprehension
1. b
2. a
3. b
4. b
5. a
6. b
7. b
8. d

Page 31
Enrichment
1. tone/setting
2. cause/effect
3. series
4. association
5. synonyms

Page 32
Graphic Development
1. Author walks into kitchen and hears noise.
2. author, cat
3. heard noise
4. The author saw the cat grin.
5. Author removes utensils, then cat.

Lesson 3
Page 33
Sentence Comprehension
1. T
2. T
3. F
4. T
5. F

Word Study
1. thump, thump
2. crunch
3. fizz
4. sssss
5. tick-tock
6. bang

Page 34
Paragraph Comprehension
1. c
2. c
3. a
4. d
5. b

Page 36
Whole-Story Comprehension
1. a
2. b
3. d
4. a
5. c
6. b
7. d
8. d

Page 37
Enrichment
1. legs like rubber
2. walk like chickens
3. hands like pieces of wood
4. fast as a steam locomotive

Page 38
Graphic Development
1. 3,000
2. male runners
3. 2,000
4. More male runners in 1997
5. 9,000

Lesson 4
Page 39
Sentence Comprehension
1. F
2. T
3. T
4. T
5. F

Word Study
1. rodeo
2. commode
3. lariat
4. mustang
5. croissants

Page 40
Paragraph Comprehension
1. c
2. b
3. a
4. d
5. c

Page 42
Whole-Story Comprehension
1. c
2. c
3. b
4. a
5. a
6. c
7. b
8. c

Page 43
Enrichment
1. I hope that I can get tickets to *Phantom of the Opera*.
2. The name of the movie showing right now is *Return of the Jedi*.
3. My favorite song right now is "Out of My Dreams," by Jo Mack.
4. *Better Homes and Gardens* has...
5. Where did you put today's issue of the *Chicago Tribune*?

Page 44
Graphic Development
1. *Girls Got It*
2. 50,000
3. *Girls Got It* Book Sales
4. It will keep dropping.
5. 20,000

Lesson 5
Page 45
Sentence Comprehension
1. F
2. T
3. T
4. F
5. T

Word Study
1. mischief
2. tomorrow
3. embarrassed
4. making
5. mysteries
6. answers

Page 46
Paragraph Comprehension
1. b
2. c
3. d
4. a
5. a

Page 48
Whole-Story Comprehension
1. d
2. b
3. c
4. a
5. a
6. c
7. a
8. c

Page 49
Enrichment
1. "I thought they were an amazing pair," said Jane.
2. "Lewis and Clark were anything but litterbugs," stated the teacher.
3. "Where did L&C start their journey?" asked Fred.
4. "L&C began in Louisiana?" questioned Sandy.
5. Mr. Roy asked, "But where did they stop?"

Page 50
Graphic Development
1. Lewis & Clark Expedition
2. St. Louis
3. Northwest
4. 13
5. Ft. Mandan, Great Falls, Fort Clatsop

Lesson 6
Page 51
Sentence Comprehension
1. T
2. F
3. T
4. T
5. F

Word Study
1. 90,000,000
2. 64,000,000
3. 25,000,000
4. 90,000,000,000
5. 2,000,000,000,000

Page 52
Paragraph Comprehension
1. a
2. d
3. c
4. c
5. b

Page 54
Whole-Story Comprehension
1. c
2. d
3. a
4. b
5. c
6. d
7. b
8. c

Page 55
Enrichment
1. G
2. F
3. E
4. H
5. B
6. D
7. A
8. I
9. C

Page 56
Graphic Development
1. Dating Dinosaurs
2. million years ago
3. Mesozoic Era
4. 2,500 to 544 mya
5. Cenozoic Era

Lesson 7
Page 57
Sentence Comprehension
1. F
2. T
3. F
4. F
5. T

Word Study
1. newspaper – paper with news on it
2. cowboy – a male who works with cows
3. hairnet – a net used to cover the head
4. homebound – heading for home

Page 58
Paragraph Comprehension
1. d
2. c
3. d
4. b
5. a

Page 60
Whole-Story Comprehension
1. d
2. a
3. b
4. c
5. d
6. a
7. c
8. b

Page 61
Enrichment
1. CD
2. megabytes

Answer Key (cont.)

3. URL, Web site
4. LEGOs
5. DVD

Page 62
Graphic Development
1. Gulf of Santa Catalina
2. north
3. CA's smaller cities
4. south
5. I-5

Lesson 8
Page 63
Sentence Comprehension
1. F   4. T
2. T   5. F
3. T

Word Study
1. g   4. e
2. d   5. h
3. b   6. a

Page 64
Paragraph Comprehension
1. c   4. a
2. b   5. b
3. c

Page 66
Whole Story Comprehension
1. b   5. a
2. d   6. d
3. b   7. c
4. b   8. a

Page 67
Enrichment
1, 3, 5

Page 68
Graphic Development
1. Parking Zone
2. No Cars
3. Both directions of traffic
4. Stop sign
5. Right turn

Lesson 9
Page 69
Sentence Comprehension
1. T   4. T
2. F   5. F
3. F

Word Study
1. Sandy
2. November
3. Grandma
4. Nan
5. Thanksgiving
6. Heidi

Page 70
Paragraph Comprehension
1. c   4. d
2. b   5. d
3. a

Page 72
Whole Story Comprehension
1. d   5. c
2. a   6. b
3. b   7. c
4. b   8. b

Page 73
Enrichment
1. positive/negative
2. positive/negative
3. negative/positive
4. negative/positive
5. positive/negative
6. positive/negative

Page 74
Graphic Development
1. Number of boys & girls playing video games from 1995–1999
2. 45 million
3. Video Game Mania
4. 15 million
5. 23 million

Lesson 10
Page 75
Sentence Comprehension
1. T   4. F
2. F   5. T
3. T

Word Study
1. amazing
2. curious
3. nutritious
4. together
5. mothering
6. sandwiches

Page 76
Paragraph Comprehension
1. d   4. b
2. a   5. c
3. b

Page 78
Whole Story Comprehension
1. d   5. c
2. c   6. b
3. a   7. a
4. a   8. d

Page 79
Enrichment
1. even
2. Because
3. Although
4. now
5. And finally

Page 80
Graphic Development
1. milk allergy
2. five more people
3. Kids with Allergies at Hualapai Elementary School
4. Pollen allergy
5. 35 people

Lesson 11
Page 81
Sentence Comprehension
1. F   4. F
2. T   5. F
3. F

Word Study
1. state of moving together
2. state of sending
3. person who places music together
4. expressing feelings

5. to place out

Page 82
Paragraph Comprehension
1. c   4. d
2. c   5. b
3. a

Page 84
Whole Story Comprehension
1. a   5. a
2. c   6. b
3. b   7. d
4. d   8. d

Page 85
Enrichment
Answers will vary.

Page 86
Graphic Development
1. straightened rivers and built canals
2. 1980s
3. Trouble in the Everglades
4. Large numbers of people began settling in Florida.
5. phosphorus

Lesson 12
Page 87
Sentence Comprehension
1. T   4. F
2. T   5. F
3. T

Word Study
1. join, unite, combine
2. question, inquire
3. naughty, evil, wicked
4. under, below
5. valiant, brave, daring
6. bright, radiant
7. summon, command
8. make, construct
9. bring, lug, transport
10. youngsters, kids

Page 88
Paragraph Comprehension
1. b   4. b
2. c   5. d
3. a

Page 90
Whole Story Comprehension
1. b   5. d
2. d   6. c
3. d   7. b
4. c   8. c

Page 91
Enrichment
1. sales
2. suspects
3. addresses
4. Beanies
5. beans
6. potatoes
7. leaves
8. deer
9. worries
10. bunches
11. teeth
12. collectors
13. messes
14. companies

15. inches
16. coaches
17. beliefs
18. thieves

Page 92
Graphic Development
1. 1998
2. Teddy
3. Mary Beth's Bean Bag World
4. The Rise and Fall of Beanies
5. $1,000

Lesson 13
Page 93
Sentence Comprehension
1. T   4. T
2. F   5. F
3. F

Word Study
1. natural
2. weakness/weaken
3. friendship
4. carelessness
5. agreeable

Page 94
Paragraph Comprehension
1. c   4. a
2. d   5. b
3. d

Page 96
Whole Story Comprehension
1. b   5. c
2. a   6. b
3. b   7. b
4. c   8. c

Page 97
Enrichment
5,1,4,2,3

Page 98
Graphic Development
1. 1 student
2. 8 students
3. Tea Cups
4. 25 students
5. none

Lesson 14
Page 99
Sentence Comprehension
1. T   4. T
2. F   5. T
3. F

Word Study
1. sparkle   4. spark
2. spat   5. sparrow
3. speak

Page 100
Paragraph Comprehension
1. b   4. a
2. d   5. b
3. c

Page 102
Whole Story Comprehension
1. b   5. c
2. d   6. a
3. b   7. c
4. c   8. b

Answer Key (cont.)

Page 103
Enrichment
1, 4, 5, 7, 8

Page 104
Graphic Development
1. 3
2. national park site
3. The Wrong Move?
4. Botswana, Namibia, Zimbabwe
5. Hluhluwe-Umfolozi

Lesson 15
Page 105
Sentence Comprehension
1. T   4. T
2. F   5. F
3. T

Word Study
1. FBI   4. IBM
2. DARE   5. IRS
3. CIA   6. NASA

Page 106
Paragraph Comprehension
1. b   4. c
2. d   5. c
3. a

Page 108
Whole-Story Comprehension
1. c   5. a
2. b   6. c
3. c   7. b
4. c   8. d

Page 109
Enrichment
1. the community itself
2. teaches an alternative to violence and delinquency
3. self-esteem, optimism, faith for the future
4. Youth Enrichment Services

Page 110
Graphic Development
1. touring dairy farms, camping, doing service projects
2. service projects
3. Super Summer Activities
4. touring dairy farms
5. Answers will vary.

Lesson 16
Page 111
Sentence Comprehension
1. T   4. F
2. F   5. F
3. T

Word Study
1. found
2. opened
3. looked
4. succeeded
5. completed
6. waited
7. chained
8. wanted

Page 112
Paragraph Comprehension
1. c   4. b
2. b   5. d
3. a

Page 114
Whole-Story Comprehension
1. b   5. a
2. c   6. a
3. d   7. d
4. c   8. b

Page 115
Enrichment
1. fish or other squid, sometimes whales
2. males get about 25 feet, females about 60 feet
3. the largest invertebrate
4. It rips chunks of flesh from the prey with its beak.
5. causes the squid to rise

Page 116
Graphic Development
1. blue whale
2. 30 feet
3. Large Animals of the Sea
4. 25 feet
5. 40 feet

Lesson 17
Page 117
Sentence Comprehension
1. F   4. T
2. F   5. T
3. F

Word Study
1. hot
2. wet
3. hard
4. heavy
5. weak
6. night
7. long, tall
8. cowardly
9. bad
10. over
11. up
12. in

Page 118
Paragraph Comprehension
1. d   4. a
2. b   5. b
3. c

Page 120
Whole-Story Comprehension
1. b   5. b
2. a   6. a
3. c   7. c
4. d   8. d

Page 121
Enrichment
1. yes
2. yes
3. proper nouns, proper adjectives
4. first words in quotation

Page 122
Graphic Development
1. the similarities and differences between *Star Wars* and *Phantom Menace*
2. Any two similarities will work.
3. *Phantom Menace*
4. computer artists
5. both

Lesson 18
Page 123
Sentence Comprehension
1. F   4. F
2. T   5. T
3. F

Word Study
1. enormous
2. small
3. fun
4. new
5. cute
6. wicked

Page 124
Paragraph Comprehension
1. b   4. c
2. c   5. d
3. b

Page 126
Whole-Story Comprehension
1. a   5. b
2. c   6. a
3. d   7. c
4. b   8. a

Page 127
Enrichment
2. graduate
3. champion
4. bicycle
5. veterinarian or veteran
6. trigonometry
7. automobile
8. mathematics
9. telephone
10. convict

Page 128
Graphic Development
1. Night in Terror Tower
2. 21 students
3. three
4. two
5. no

Lesson 19
Page 129
Sentence Comprehension
1. F   4. F
2. T   5. T
3. F

Word Study
1. hyper   6. semi
2. inter   7. hexa
3. cir   8. intro
4. cata   9. inter
5. co   10. extra

Page 130
Paragraph Comprehension
1. b   4. d
2. a   5. b
3. c

Page 132
Whole-Story Comprehension
1. d   5. c
2. c   6. b
3. a   7. c
4. c   8. d

Page 133
Enrichment
1. series of words
2. to set off dialogue
3. between two clauses

Page 134
Graphic Development
1. Characters from *Harry Potter and the Sorcerer's Stone*
2. Albus Dumbledore
3. 3
4. On Harry's side, twice as tall as men
5. Harry Potter

Lesson 20
Page 135
Sentence Comprehension
1. T   4. F
2. T   5. F
3. F

Word Study
1. inches
2. miles
3. centimeters
4. yards
5. feet
6. decimeters

Page 136
Paragraph Comprehension
1. a   4. b
2. c   5. c
3. b

Page 138
Whole-Story Comprehension
1. c   5. d
2. b   6. a
3. b   7. a
4. c   8. b

Page 139
Enrichment
1. blue, humpback, and minke whales
2. baleen whales don't have teeth.
3. 34 mph
4. blue whale
5. humpback whale

Page 140
Graphic Development
1. Western side
2. North Atlantic Ocean, east
3. Pacific Ocean
4. south
5. Arctic

Answer Sheet

Directions: Fill in the bubble of the correct answer "a," "b," "c," "d," or "e" on this sheet. If the answer is "True," fill in the "a" bubble, and if the answer is "False," fill in the "b" bubble.